CASE STUDIES IN
EDUCATION AND CULTURE

General Editors

GEORGE and LOUISE SPINDLER

Stanford University

ENCULTURATION AND SOCIALIZATION IN AN IJAW VILLAGE

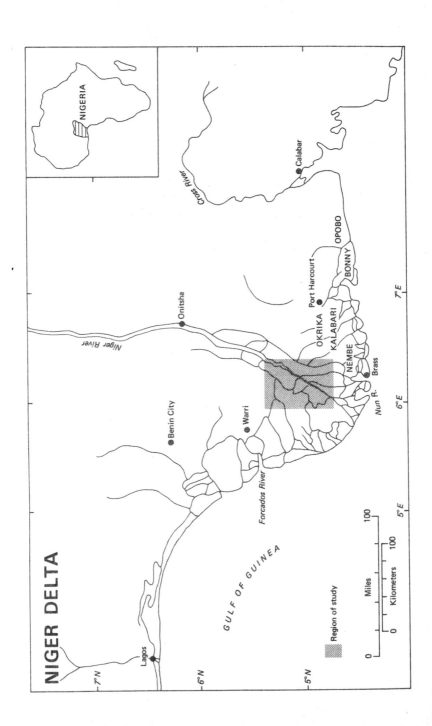

ENCULTURATION AND SOCIALIZATION IN AN IJAW VILLAGE

PHILIP E. LEIS

IRVINGTON PUBLISHERS, INC.
551 FIFTH AVENUE NEW YORK, N.Y. 10017

First Irvington Edition 1984

Copyright ©1972 by Holt, Rinehart & Winston

Library of Congress Cataloging in Publication Data

Leis, Philip E.
     Enculturation and socialization in an Ijaw village.

     (Case studies in cultural anthropology)
     Reprint. Originally published: New York : Holt, Rinehart and Winston, c1972. (Case studies in education and culture)
     Bibliography: p.
     Includes index.
     1. Ijo (Agrican people) 2. Socialization--Case studies. 3. Children--Nigeria. I. Title.
II. Series. III. Series: Case studies in education and culture.
(DT515.45.I35L44   1983)   306'.08996   82-7160

ISBN 0-8290-0710-5 (pbk.)

Printed in the United States of America

Foreword

About the Series

This series brings to students the results of direct observation and participation in educational process, by anthropologists, in a variety of cultural settings, including some within the contemporary United States. Each of the books in this series is selected as an enduring example of educational anthropology. Classrooms, schools, communities and their schools, cultural transmission in societies where there are no schools in the Western sense, all are represented in the series. The authors of these studies move beyond formalistic treatments of institutions to the interaction among the people engaged in educative events, their thinking and feeling, and to the educative transactions themselves.

Education is a cultural process. Every act of teaching and learning is a cultural event. Education recruits new members into society and maintains the culture. Education may also be an instrument for change as new adaptations are disseminated.

Generalizations about relationships between schools and communities, education and society, and education and culture become meaningful when education is studied as a cultural process. This series is intended for use in courses in education, and in anthropology and the other social sciences, where these relationships are particularly relevant. They will stimulate thinking and discussion about education that is not confined by one's own cultural experience. The cross-cultural emphasis of the series is particularly significant. Without this perspective, our view will be obscured by ethnocentric bias.

About the Author

Philip Leis received his B.A. at Antioch College and his Ph.D. in anthropology from Northwestern University in 1962. He is Associate Professor and Chairman of the Anthropology Department at Brown University. From 1960 to 1962 he taught at Iowa State University. He has published several papers based on his fieldwork with the Washo Indians in Nevada, the Ijaw in Nigeria, and the Nyam-Nyam in the Cameroon.

About the Book

This is a study of the way Ijaw educate their children to behave and believe in the life style of Ijaw society and culture. During the period 1957 to 1959, the author lived in the central part of the Niger Delta where cultural change in a village had been slow because of its geographical isolation from the mainland. His objectives were to study Ijaw educational patterns, the processes of enculturation and socialization, and to relate these to changes occurring in Ijaw culture during recent times.

By contrasting the Ijaw with the Kanuri of Bornu, described by Alan Peshkin in this same series, the reader can grasp some of the complexity of the multi-ethnic Nigerian situation. Both studies center on the educational process, though Peshkin's describes the results of the introduction of an alien educational system, while the Ijaw case stresses the indigenous educational system.

The Ijaw case study is notable for its attention to a problem of considerable significance to those interested in child development—the early learning hypothesis. Its value, however, does not rest on the investigation of this topic alone. By describing the culture of a little known society, the study also provides data both for understanding the constituency of one of the largest African nations and for cross-cultural comparisons of education and cultural change.

George and Louise Spindler
General Editors

Phlox, Wisconsin

Preface

Because of its location in the center of the Niger Delta, Ebiama, the Ijaw village described in the following pages, was isolated from most of the historical events affecting mainland Nigeria. Innovations had been introduced and accepted slowly, but with the approach of independence, scheduled for October 1, 1960, the villagers anticipated that the rate of change would increase rapidly. They were not certain, however, whether the changes would be the type they wanted. In the glow of nascent nationhood many felt uneasy about the possibility of a return to "intertribal wars," or, more accurately, to intervillage feuds. Those days were not remembered as a Golden Age, though the past could barely foretell the havoc of the Nigeria-Biafra War that would follow within a few years. This study looks forward to a time when the Ijaw will have the opportunity to adapt the educational processes of acquiring Ijaw culture and becoming a member of Ijaw society to the new alternatives open within a developing nation.

Ijaw living in the Delta and in mainland cities were generous with their hospitality and time in discussing their way of life. Their patience in trying to enculturate and socialize two strangers is gratefully acknowledged. In Ebiama, I. Kigibie and Mr. and Mrs. R. Akigha were unstinting as tutors, assistants, and friends. Though data from other Ijaw communities are not presented here, I wish to thank Jacob Cameron, Sinclair Amatare, Gideon Oki, Ogbo Ariye, and Foyowei Ogbowah for their assistance when we visited or resided in their villages. In addition, I am grateful to the staff of the Nigerian Institute of Social and Economic Research at Ibadan; Richard Franklin and Alan Runickles, District Officers at Brass; Dr. T. O. na Oruwariye at Ibadan; and John S. Boston, then Curator of the Nigerian Museum at Lagos, and his wife for their consideration. Robin Horton was not only magnanimous in welcoming us to the Ijaw and pointing out that our study of the Western Ijaw would complement his anthropological research with the Kalabari in the eastern Delta, he did everything possible to facilitate our entry into the Delta.

Professor Melville J. Herskovits advised the writing of the doctoral dissertation at Northwestern University from which the present work is partly derived. My intellectual debt to him will be evident in both the selection of topic and the analysis of data. I am also indebted to Professors William R. Bascom for having first suggested the Ijaw for study, Edward P. Dozier for directing my attention to the "early learning hypothesis," and Paul J. Bohannan, Edward M. Bruner, James W. Fernandez, Francis L. K. Hsu, Igor Kopytoff, and Robert A. LeVine for reading parts of earlier drafts of this work and contributing valuable suggestions. Professors Niels W. Braroe and George L. Hicks read the complete manuscript and additional revisions were made on the basis of their comments.

Research in England and Nigeria from October 1957 to July 1959 was supported by The Ford Foundation as part of its African Area Training Fellowship Program. I also appreciate the grants awarded by Brown University and the National Institute of Mental Health that allowed me additional time for writing.

Finally, this study could not have proceeded without the discernment of Nancy B. Leis in recording relevant Ijaw data on women and children. Of course, I alone am responsible for whatever shortcomings are to be found here.

Philip E. Leis

Providence, R.I.

Contents

1 / Introduction

BIAMA[1] IS AN AVERAGE-SIZED IJAW VILLAGE of about 700 people. The houses are built on the high banks of a waterway, but distant views are cut off because the stream is narrow and twists sharply allowing the forest to encroach on all sides. The environment, aided by historical events, both causes and symbolizes the isolation of the village. Elderly Ijaw know little of what goes on beyond the village, and still less of the world beyond the Delta. The term "Nigeria," for example, must be translated to them by naming cities on the mainland to convey the sense of a large territory. Younger people, particularly those who went or are going to school, are more aware of the facts of history and geography. They know what is meant by Nigeria; they also know, since the Headmaster of the local school has a radio, that rockets are fired toward the moon. Their understanding and interpretation of these facts and many more, however, are limited by their experience. By contrast, events in the village are easily visible and an understanding of them is self-evident to all the inhabitants.

The comparison of the open village to the closed surrounding environment is intended to be a relative rather than an absolute measure. Just as children are far from being totally ignorant of affairs foreign to their village, so they are not privy to everything that happens within its boundaries. There are certain secret rituals, for example, from which children are excluded; but generally, until they are old enough to comprehend the meaning of adult behavior, their childhood is hedged in only by the nature of their own ineptitudes.

To describe Ebiama as "open" implies two aspects of community life. One is the layout of the village. Houses are close to each other with no walls or other obstructions between them. Each has a verandah in front on which meals are eaten and guests are entertained. Since children spend most of their time playing or working outside, they can do few things without being overheard or seen by kinsmen or passersby. Everyone is also free to observe rituals performed in most of the cult-houses. The accessibility of social activities interrelates with the second meaning of an open community: what people do in private often becomes widespread knowledge. Through gossip, fights, court cases, and propitiation of the deities, events inside houses or secretly performed elsewhere are eventually brought to public view. These revelations produce subtle disapprobation by fellow community

---

[1] Of the twenty months spent in the Delta, we resided for close to a year here. Village, clan, and personal names are pseudonyms.

A view looking down river.

Two brothers, close to ninety years of age, who are the oldest men in the village.

Ijaw in a canoe, imitating the way men dressed and left for war in the "old" days.

members and combine with fear of punishment by the deities to constitute the principal restraints necessary for social existence. They provide the basis for social control in a society finely balanced between individual independence and social interdependence.

"Free" choice in Ijaw ideology and practice is found to be a repetitive theme in economic, social, political, and religious institutions. Within the context of possibilities shaped by Ijaw history, individuals believe they have several alternatives open to them, and the range of choice has been enlarged by changes around and within the community. Village elders unknowingly voice the clichés heard in societies around the world about life changing too rapidly. Their complaint often centers on a younger generation that seems to be failing to emulate traditional Ijaw ways of life.

Traditional Ijaw culture, of course, exists only insofar as the Ijaw themselves believe their customs are the same as those practiced by their ancestors. Without written records it is impossible to prove conclusively that a belief or practice has not changed through time; indeed, logic and assumptions derived from anthropological theories of cultural change would lead us to conclude the opposite. Beliefs affirmed by elders, however, contrast with some of the behavior of young adults who seek, but do not always accept, innovations. For the latter, change has not happened fast enough and they resent the conditions that have kept them isolated from the economic and political developments occurring in the rest of Nigeria.

From our perspective both generations have, to a certain extent, objective perceptions of reality. The old people sense rapid change because within their lifetimes Europeans first entered the area. New political institutions, Christianity, and schooling were introduced, and the Ijaw became inextricably tied to a money economy. Younger people who desire change are also correct, on their part, in estimating the slower rate of development in the Delta than on the mainland. People in the cities have political power; they have more schools and health centers; and they reap the benefits of full participation in the national economy. According to the views of old and young, history and environment played a foul trick on the Delta peoples, especially by allowing other ethnic groups whom their ancestors claimed as slaves to achieve positions of prominence.

To an outside observer Ebiama is an ongoing Ijaw community where the generational differences in attitudes toward change are slight compared to the consensual core of Ijaw values. Innovations have been introduced slowly and are practiced by a part of the village population or they are frequently accepted without loss of the traditional cultural forms by the same people. Why does differential change occur? Many answers have been proposed for similar situations in various parts of the world. In this book we wish to investigate the suggestion that educational experiences strongly influence cultural and social persistence or instability, particularly during acculturation when opportunities for change become available.

EDUCATION, ENCULTURATION, AND SOCIALIZATION

Education refers to the total process of learning that extends to all organisms whose behaviors are shaped by some form of learned adaptation to their environment rather than by heredity alone. Schooling is the formalized procedure for learning. All human societies must educate their young since culture cannot be genetically transferred, but schools are not found in all societies since education can proceed informally. The two terms have also been contrasted by their role in stimulating change. Schools are called either agents of conservatism or the vanguards of change. Depending on the place and time, they can be both by passing on accumulated knowledge of the past and by stimulating new ideas for the future. Education connotes a more static quality because the perpetuation of society depends upon it. In Ebiama the school symbolizes change because it is associated with Christianity and foreign innovations. What is learned in school becomes part of the education of Ijaw children, but this knowledge is a small, and often unrelated, part of their total education acquired in Ijaw society. As a result of this difference, the school has had a minimal impact on the community thus far.

Enculturation and socialization, two other terms used to delineate the relationship between education and change, have not been as sharply distinguished from each other as education and schooling. As Margaret Mead observes, the tendency to make them one and the same thing has resulted in the function of education being misunderstood and misinterpreted (Mead 1963). She defines socialization as "the set of species-wide requirements and exactions made on human beings by human societies," and enculturation as "the process of learning a culture in all its uniqueness and particularity" (1963:187).

Herskovits' definition of socialization is similar to Mead's, but enculturation to him is a distinctive factor in cultural change: ". . . at the earliest stages of human existence [enculturation] contributes to social stability and cultural continuity . . . while the process, as it is operative on more mature folk, is highly important in inducing change" (1947:40–41).

The confusion created by different definitions of these terms might by resolved by drawing a correspondence between them and the concepts of culture and society. If society is conceptualized as a set of patterned interactions, and culture as a system of symbols—and for human societies the empirical referents of one cannot exist without the other—then socialization is the process of learning how to behave in a particular society (contrary to Mead's definition), and enculturation is the process of acquiring a world view. Since societal variations seem limited in scope because of the biophysical requirements of man, socialization practices are more comparable to each other cross-culturally than are enculturative patterns, given man's great capacity for symbolic variation. To ensure that the interplay between the two processes is studied, enculturation and socialization should not be defined synonymously.

It must be emphasized that these two concepts are abstractions from the same material data; both refer to processes that humanize individuals. One mistake resulting from a failure to recognize this point has been the attempt to relate personality types to socialization practices without considering enculturation (Mead 1963). We will avoid questions of personality and limit our analysis to Ijaw enculturation and socialization, but parenthetically, we may observe in the hypothesis discussed below that if what is learned earliest in life proves most stable during acculturation, this effect helps to explain why personality structure changes less readily than overt cultural behavior.[2]

Bruner and Spiro independently proposed a hypothesis—"the early learning hypothesis"—that integrates the processes of enculturation (chronological, differential change) and of acculturation (spatial, differential change). Appreciating that both psychoanalytic and learning theories accentuate the importance of primacy in personal experience, Bruner suggests that knowledge and behavior traditionally learned and internalized in infancy and early childhood tend to be more resistant to change in contact situations (Bruner 1956:197). Spiro, using the analogy of an onion, offers the same hypothesis: the first traits learned will be the inner core of experience and therefore the last to be "peeled" off during acculturation (1955: 1249). Both Bruner and Spiro emphasize the reason for traits remaining stable. The obverse, however, as Herskovits indicates in his definition of enculturation, should also hold true: the traits learned later in life should be least stable and the first to be shed in contact situations. Similarly, early learning in socialization can be hypothesized to effect social change. We anticipate that traits of social behavior like those of culture will be flexible or inflexible relative to the age at which they are learned.

Spiro shows how acculturation might alter this expectation. Notwithstanding his onion-peeling analogy, he refers to children as important acculturative agents. He states, "If, in the normal course of social life, parents are the agents of cultural

[2] A. Irving Hallowell, *Culture and Experience,* Philadelphia: University of Pennsylvania Press, 1955, p. 334.

continuity, in acculturation children become the agents of cultural change—it is the children who teach the new culture to their parents" (1955:1247). He cites immigrants to the United States and their children as providing abundant evidence for this observation.

Regarding an acculturative situation, Spiro thus proposes: first, what is learned earliest is retained the longest, and second, children become acculturated faster than their elders. The question of whether early learning acts as stabilizer or stimulus for change depends to the largest extent on the type of acculturation experienced by the group. Do the external stimuli apply equally to the population as a whole or only to a certain age segment? In the case of acculturation in Ebiama, we have already observed that the school has thus far had a minor impact on the community at large. As with some American Indian groups, the early learning hypothesis can be examined only in acculturative situations in which the children remain comparatively more isolated from contacts than their parents, with new alternatives being filtered to them through adults in their own society.[3]

Enculturation and socialization are not intended to be simple causal explanations for cultural and social change. Bruner states that the age of learning a trait would affect its "potential resistance to change," but he also recognizes the limited explanatory value of the early learning hypothesis in that "the actual sequence of change is dependent upon a multiplicity of factors in the contact situation" (1956:196). Although the hypothesis in one form or another has been stated in a general way several times besides those already mentioned,[4] only by analyses of particular groups will we determine whether the hypothesis has even a limited application, or whether, as Wolfe claims (1961:147), the relationship between early learning and stable elements is simply fortuitous.

By providing a detailed description of Ijaw childhood, we intend not only to examine this hypothesis but also to contribute to the comparative literature on child rearing. Africa alone has produced outstanding descriptions of indigenous educational systems (for example, Fortes 1938; Raum 1940; Read 1959), but the generalization persists that anthropologists frequently neglect to describe what children learn at various ages (Henry 1960:290).

ASSUMPTIONS AND METHODS

An ethnographic account of childhood raises special problems in the description and analysis of data that are particularly relevant to the early learning hypothesis and to the distinction between enculturation and socialization. The first problem concerns "traits" or the units of study. Instead of entering the debate on the definition of a trait per se, we will proceed heuristically on the basis of the

---

[3] Shimahara's discussion of enculturation (1970) appeared after this manuscript was completed. His emphasis on the conscious nature of enculturation during childhood underlines the methodological consideration made here.

[4] M. J. Herskovits, "Education and Cultural Dynamics," *The American Journal of Sociology*, 1943, *48*, 6:737–749; A. L. Kroeber, *Anthropology* (rev. ed.), N.Y.: Harcourt, Brace & Co., 1948, pp. 347–348; F. F. Keesing, *Cultural Anthropology*, N.Y.: Rinehart & Co., 1958, p. 412.

following two assumptions: 1) Traits can be observable forms of physical behavior or unobservable ideas or values expressed in language.[5] The first type of trait we will refer to as a "behavioral" trait and consider it to be a part of socialization, in contrast to the second type which will be called an "ideational" trait and an element of enculturation. 2) Traits can be learned at differential rates during the course of a lifetime. Thus, a child might learn a particular habit by imitation (a behavioral trait) at one age, while acquiring an understanding of the sanctions underlying the physical behavior (an ideational trait) at another age.

A Seminar on Acculturation, assessing old and new directions in studies of culture change, pointed to a similar distinction in acculturative situations by advancing the proposition that:

> . . . the conventional categories of cultural description . . . do not readily lend themselves to an analysis of differential change. All cultural segments have their concrete aspects, and these more explicit behaviors and apparatus are as a rule more readily mastered than symbolic and valuational aspects.[6]

The same difference between explicit behaviors and apparatus, and symbolic and valuational aspects, would logically be as true of education as of acculturation. This assumption, however, introduces a possible contradiction between the Seminar's statement and the early learning hypothesis. According to the latter, the traits learned first should be *more* resistant to change in an acculturative situation than those learned later. Yet, concrete traits might be expected to be learned earlier in life than valuational ones, and the Seminar indicates these would be *less* resistant to change.

The definitions we offer for behavioral and ideational traits diverge somewhat from the division of cultural segments proposed by the Seminar; behavioral traits may be more "concrete" than valuational ones, but they are not necessarily more explicit. An ideational trait can be more explicit than behavior to the extent that it is well known and agreed upon by the entire community, while the behavioral expression of this sanction may vary greatly from individual to individual and thus lose its explicit nature for the community as a whole. By analyzing the stability or instability of each type of trait in Ebiama, the contradiction between the hypothesis of early learning and the proposition of the Seminar on Acculturation may be clarified, throwing the processes underlying cultural and social change into greater relief.

Relating traits to children's ages raises several other problems. In order to compare traits it is necessary to group individuals according to age. The Ijaw do not divide their life cycle into well-defined periods, terminologically or ritually. Nonetheless, we find that a number of traits cluster together for certain ages and, although traits are analytical units, they are not completely arbitrary because the units are describable and real to Ijaw. Age-periods, then, are inductively derived and form divisions in the life span: birth to the age of four, five to eight, nine to

---

[5] ". . . all culture elements have form, i.e., directly observable qualities, and also meaning, i.e., a series of associations in the minds of the group" (Ralph Linton, *Acculturation in Seven American Indian Tribes,* Gloucester, Mass.: Peter Smith, 1963 [orig. pub. 1940], p. 476).

[6] Social Science Research Council Seminar on Acculturation, 1953, "Acculturation: An Exploratory Formulation," *American Anthropologist,* 1954, 56, 6:973–1002 (pp. 990–991).

thirteen, and fourteen to seventeen. The criteria for each division will be explained in the respective following chapters.

A second problem is to set a dividing line between early and late learning. Bruner states that the Mandan-Hidatsa children learned their kinship at an "early age," that is, "between the ages six to ten," while the age-grade system was learned late: "The age-grade society was not even entered by an individual until the age seven to eight, and serious social activity did not begin for a boy until the age of fifteen to seventeen . . ." (1956:195). Without generalizing cross-culturally about what must at best be an arbitrary line of division, we draw this line for Ebiama by regarding everything learned younger than nine years old as "early," and everything acquired later than eight as "late." It is approximately at this dividing point that Ijaw children must accept responsibility for taking care of a younger sibling during the day and thereby begin to lose the status of child themselves.

A third problem is a practical aspect of the first two: how can the specific age at which an individual acquires a particular trait be determined? Ordinarily, when a parent or older sibling shows a child an activity, how to sweep the floor, for example, the child is mature enough to perform it. Here the age of being taught and the age of acting are coincidental. Even simple examples become complicated, however, by considering the obvious possibility that a child may learn how to sweep by watching his mother long before he is physically capable or required to do so. Complex learning situations, those excluding any type of explicit instructions, are even more difficult to pinpoint. If a child sits with his family members during their discussion of a problem, has he learned something about behavior toward his kinsmen, even though he is personally ignored? Performance alone obviously cannot be the sole measure of knowledge. To attempt to control for these difficulties, we noted the exposure of children in Ebiama at various age levels to elements of their culture, as well as the verbal interpretations the children could give of their learning experiences. We also attended sessions of each class at the school.

Besides extensive observations and informal interviews of both children and parents, we intensively questioned close to sixty boys and girls between the ages of five and seventeen. There was a total of 222 children in this age range; those chosen included all the children from one section of the village, as well as a few from each of the other village sections. Each child was questioned at least twice with an interval of a month or more between interviews. At one meeting he was asked questions of a hypothetical nature to elicit his opinion on how he thought he would respond in certain situations. His answer, we suspected, would be a description of his own experience. In the other session, as a cross-check, he was asked about similar events but was requested to relate facts. Although a somewhat similar sampling technique has been used by Whiting *et al.* to record variables relevant to personality studies,[7] the primary objective of the interviews was to delineate the cultural knowledge of each child.

---

[7] John W. M. Whiting *et al.*, *Field Manual for the Cross-Cultural Study of Child Rearing.* New York: Social Science Research Council, 1953 (mimeographed).

Ijaw usually express age in relative terms so that one is always a "small child" (*kala tọbọu*)[8] to those older than oneself. Nevertheless, their practice of placing individuals born within a few months of each other into age-groups enabled us to approximate the age of a boy or girl. Ages were checked with written records kept by a few parents and from parents able to recall birthdays in relation to recorded events.

Living in a house located in the middle of the village permitted us to take full advantage of the open view to community life of adults as well as children. Chapter 2 offers an historical and ethnographic resumé of the community, indicating the areas in which social and cultural changes have occurred. The problem of differential change is taken up again in Chapters 8 and 9 in the context of the prenatal and childhood periods detailed in Chapters 3 to 7. The present tense is used to describe Ebiama as it was at the time of our study in 1958–1959. The past tense, except in illustrations of particular events, is reserved for recorded history and traditions remembered by Ijaw but no longer practiced by anyone in the village.

---

[8] Two vowels in succession indicate a diphthong; *o* equals the English o as in owe; *ọ* equals a as in awful; *e* is equivalent to the French é or English ei as in neighbor; *ẹ* equals e as in wet. Definitions of Ijaw words and of specialized anthropological terms are found in the Glossary.

2 / Ebiama

BOTH TRADITIONAL AND INNOVATIVE ASPECTS of Ebiama culture and society are described in this chapter to provide a framework for the subsequent chapters on education. The introductory comments on location and history are followed by sections on primary familial units, including the closely related processes of inheritance and marriage, and on economics, political organization, and religion.

LOCATION

Ebiama lies along the Ikebiri Creek a couple of miles above the mangroves, approximately five degrees north of the equator, in what was called at the time of this study the Eastern Region of Nigeria. It is somewhat more isolated than other central Delta villages because the shallow stream is inaccessible to craft larger than canoes. As a consequence, government officials who travel in launches rarely visit the village. Furthermore, since the village is several hours away by canoe from the Nun River, a main artery of the Niger, and does not have a market place, there is little to attract strangers. The nearest neighboring community requires a journey of slightly less than a half hour. The only village with a land connection to Ebiama is about five miles distant, but the path traverses swamps that make it virtually impassable during the rainy season.

Although few visitors, especially non-Ijaw ones, venture to this area, many residents of Ebiama travel widely. They trade at markets in the Delta and at cities, such as Warri, Port Harcourt, and Onitsha, accessible by canoe. Palm oil products are carried to a village on the Nun River for sale to a United Africa Company station. Fishing expeditions go out to the nearby mangroves and to places as far away as Lagos or the Cameroons. Their sojourns in fishing settlements are usually with relatives and other Ijaw. Unlike Ijaw from coastal towns, few men from Ebiama have taken permanent employment on the mainland as domestics for Europeans or as unskilled laborers in urban areas.

Even though the trips have had little acculturative effect, traveling has had important consequences for the economy, since production and consumption are tied through trade to the Nigerian mainland and to foreign markets. This is not a recent development, for external trade has taken place over a period of hundreds of years; what is new during the lifetime of village elders is the opportunity to travel without fear of being robbed or captured by pirates for sale into slavery. Until the Pax Britannica, traveling was dangerous even in nearby areas because of intervillage wars. Village sovereignty in the central area emphasized dissociation from other communities, and this condition was compounded by the Ijaw organizations that formed in the eastern part of the Delta.

HISTORIC CONTEXT

The Ijaw living in the Niger Delta never constituted a single political society.[1] Most of them had social organizations extending only to their village boundaries, and this dissection into village units closely mirrored the physiography of the Delta. A narrow sandy beach along the coast introduces a mangrove belt fifteen to thirty miles wide. On the other side of the mangroves the land begins a steady rise, built up by the annual flooding of the Niger River. Throughout these three zones, streams and rivers crisscross making the mouth of the Niger look like an intricately woven Ijaw fishing net.

Most Ijaw believe that they are all descended from an ancestor by the name of Ijǫ who fled from Benin during a civil war and settled in the Niger Delta. Ancestry has been pushed further back by a few literate Ijaw who reason that Ila-Ife or Egypt must be the point of origin for their people. One writer casts farther afield, claiming Noah for paterfamilias and thereby accounting for the etymology of an Ijaw term of greeting, *noao* (Owunaro 1949:18). The most realistic alternatives suggested by oral traditions and cultural similarities between Ijaw and mainland groups are that the ancestor or ancestors of the Ijaw entered the Delta from the direction of the Benin Kingdom (Leonard 1906:30; Welch 1937:4; Dike 1956:23) or of Igboland (Talbot 1932:5). The Ijaw have occupied the Delta since at least the fifteenth century when travelers report encounters with them, and probably much earlier considering the linguistic classification of Ijaw that places it as a separate language or subdivision of Kwa within the Niger-Congo language family.[2]

The shared belief in common descent, supported by linguistic and cultural affinities, provided the basis for some political cohesion at the time national politics became important. This nascent development of unity, however, stems more from a reaction to competition with other ethnic groups than from historical traditions. Exceptions are found in the eastern part of the Delta where trading contacts encouraged the formation of five large complex political organizations or "clans."

These clans—Nembe, Kalabari, Okrika, Bonny, and Opobo—contained "Houses," called *wari,* that dominated the trade first in slaves and then in palm oil between Europeans and the hinterland peoples for close to four centuries (Dike 1956:24; Horton 1960:8). In the sixteenth century, the Houses were trading concerns, composed of traders, their families, and slaves. The original forms may have resembled the social organization of Ebiama and other villages found in the central Delta

---

[1] Other names and spellings include Ijǫ, Ijoh, Ejoe, Jo, and Oru. According to the 1952–1953 Nigerian Census, there were 305,850 Ijaw living in the Delta.

[2] Joseph H. Greenberg, *The Languages of Africa.* The Hague: Mouton & Co., and Bloomington: Indiana University, 1963.

at present. Within the next two centuries, the eastern clans gained enormous economic sophistication and political power, giving Dike reason to characterize them as "city-states" (1956:31). The clans used their positions near the mouths of navigable rivers to act as middlemen for the Europeans who preferred to remain on their ships and enjoy the sea breezes. Houses within these polities rose and fell in competition with each other and in response to the ascension and demise of talented leaders, but they were able to maintain their strategic positions by force of arms and by exploiting divisiveness among the foreign trading companies until the end of the nineteenth century (Jones 1963; Alagoa 1964).

Early reports from European travelers imply that even without the strategies of the eastern clans Ijaw living in other parts of the Delta were unwilling to enter into direct trading relationships. Ijaw were thought to be a "predatory race,"[3] and Richard Lander, after discovering the egress of the Niger River, was killed at Angiama.[4] This village is located only several hours by canoe from Ebiama. British administrative reports as late as 1926 on the Ijaw living just to the west of Ebiama noted that the " 'truculent Ijaws' had 'never really been conquered.' " In the same year, the European trading companies complained to the Government about the "piracy" of the Ijaw (cited by Ikime 1967:75). Subsequent to pacification, the Western Ijaw tended to reverse their position and welcomed modern government and economic development. They came finally to the point of complaining about lack of governmental attention to their region (Ikime 1967).

ASPECTS OF FAMILY ORGANIZATION

Residence and Descent Groups   An emphasis on individual choice, found in economic, political, and religious behavior, plays an important part in the social organization of the community. Despite the expressed preference for patrilocal residence, Ijaw men reside in several different places before finally settling down, and often those places are not with their fathers. Women move because on marrying they must go to their husbands' domiciles. This movement, confirmed by life histories and census data, gives the appearance of Ijaw having innumerable alternatives as to where to live and with whom to have social relationships. The choices turn out to be limited by several factors, but the residential groupings still show a great flexibility in living arrangements.

Residential shifts also point to a long range historical phenomenon that is described by oral histories and helps to explain the process by which the Delta may have been settled. Conflicts between villages and disputes between individuals of the same family usually resulted in a move of one or more of them to new areas. Within a generation, or even more quickly if other families should join a new settlement, a village (*ama*) would have formed. Since migrations often were only to nearby areas, the notions of kinship and village affinities became intertwined.

---

[3] J. Adams, *Remarks on the Country Extending from Cape Palmas to the River Congo,* London, 1823, p. 117.

[4] W. B. Baikie, *Narrative of an Exploring Voyage up the Rivers Kwora and Binue in 1854,* London, 1856, p. 36.

Theoretically, only those villages founded by descendants of a common ancestor can be parts of the same *ibe*. In practice, the Ijaw believe an *ibe* includes everyone who professes descent from a common ancestor; actually being able to trace connections to him is unnecessary. When emigrants settled too far away from their home village to maintain contacts, the members of the new village, through intermarriage and assimilation to local cultural differences, tended over several generations to formulate a pseudo-history to substantiate their affiliation with the nearest *ibe*. Under British rule the process was encouraged because *ibe* were defined as "clans" and became the basic territorial groupings for administrative purposes.

Opuama *ibe,* of which the people of Ebiama believe themselves to be a part, exemplifies the peripheral importance of the *ibe* to its members in past times. Opuama literally means "village of Opu" and may reflect an historical period when all the descendants of Opu lived in one place. According to oral histories recorded in 1931 by the District Officer, Opu was one of the sons of Rotoma, founder of a neighboring *ibe,* who had "dropped out of a cloud." Because of a desecration, Opu fled from his father's village and settled in the area now referred to as Opuama. There was some question about the relationship of Ebiebi, the founder of Ebiama, to the other village founders, and the District Officer concluded that he was probably an immigrant from the western part of the Delta. Nonetheless, all the Opuama villages were considered by the government to be part of Rotoma Clan.

Within thirty years the inhabitants have come to profess a new history. The founder of Opuama now is considered a direct descendant of Ijǫ, and the founders of five of the six villages comprising the territory are thought to be the sons of Opu. The people in the sixth village say they immigrated recently to their present location. The reformulation records the desire of Opuama members to be recognized as a clan separate from Rotoma in the modern framework of government. This separation was accepted by the Nigerian government.

No land was held in the name of the *ibe* and those who belonged to it never waged war or defended themselves as a group. Most armed encounters recalled by elders in Ebiama were between segments of the *ibe*. Members of the *ibe* acted together only to worship a particular deity, believed to have come with Opu in his travels to the area. Although the deity is still referred to in a respectful tone in some of the villages, it has not "chosen" a priest for many years and therefore does not cause the *ibe* members to worship it. Because of its dormancy, the people of Ebiama largely ignore it in practice and belief.

The *ibe,* then, aside from being the basis for modern-day political groupings, seems to have been more the result than the cause of placing outside limits on social relationships and cultural affinities. Social relationships, including conflicts, are based on proximity. With more opportunities for meeting *ibe* members than people from distant areas, and since most other Ijaw *ibe* practice clitoridectomy, an abhorrent custom in Opuama, endogamous marriages occur without recourse to a specified rule of marriage preference.[5] Thus, close to 93 percent of the married or widowed women living in Ebiama are from the village itself or from other

---

[5] According to an Ijaw belief, clitoridectomy was performed in Opuama until one time when seven girls died after the operation.

Opuama villages. Cultural similarities result from this intermixture, and circularly, the shared beliefs promote social contacts. Nevertheless, since the extension of significant social and political ties to the *ibe* occurred intensively only in recent times, the largest perimeter of social importance remains at the level of the village.

Ebiama consists of five sections which are divided into subsections. Each of these divisons is named: three of the sections for the sons, presumably, of Ebiebi; the other two sections for their geographical position; and the subsections for those descendants who had large enough families for their portion of the section to become identified with them. Although there are no fences or other physical markers between subsections and sections, should a knowledgeable Ijaw wish to draw boundaries, he could separate them with fairly straight lines running from the river to the forest behind the village.

There are five to fifteen households in a subsection and an average of thirty households to a section. Houses are rectangular, built with wattle and daub walls, and thatch roofs. The plans of dwellings vary slightly in design, but all provide each wife with her own living quarters. They are located on either side of a central room used by the husband for receiving guests or next to each other and to one side of the main room. A woman, then, has her own sleeping room and kitchen, but she does not normally live in an entirely separate dwelling from her co-wives, as is the typical practice in many African societies. Ordinarily, a husband alternates sleeping in the apartments of his wives and does not have his own bedroom. Young children sleep with their mothers; older ones move into vacant rooms wherever available.

The ideal type household contains a man, his wives, and their unmarried children. In practice there are many variations. A woman and her children might live apart from her husband because his house lacks space or is in need of repairs, situations sometimes resulting in her residing for several years in a nearby house. A widowed or divorced woman may be living with her parents, with her married children, or by herself until she remarries. The husband and one of his wives may have children by a previous marriage living with them, or children of divorced parents could reside with their paternal or maternal grandparents. Young unmarried siblings or children of siblings might also be members of a household. These are some of the reasons why only 60 percent of the children in Ebiama live with both their biological parents.[6]

Within a subsection of the village all the heads of households are related to each other because they can reckon descent through male or female links to its eponymous founder. Descent lines cannot be traced precisely since the genealogical depth to the founder may be more than seven or eight generations. But at the very least the kinsmen in the second ascending generation are known, and each of them resided where he did because of his grandparents having lived there, and so on back to the founder. Stated another way, Ijaw have the right to reside in any part of Ebiama or other villages founded by an ancestor if their consanguineous kinsmen live or have lived in the subsection named for him.

---

[6] Of 371 children under age 17, 227 live with both parents, 72 with their mother, 25 with their father, and 47 with other relatives.

The intermeshing of village organization and kinship, which constitutes the framework for residential choices, is illustrated by the Ijaw terminology in the following diagrams:

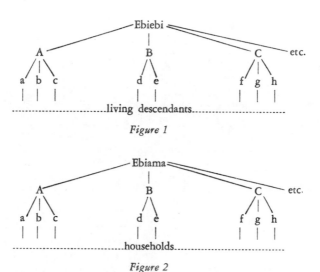

Figure 1

Figure 2

In abbreviated forms, Figure 1 represents all the descendants of Ebiebi and Figure 2 the structure of the village. Capital letters indicate the descendants for whom sections are named; lower case letters are for founders of subsections. The duplication of letters in the two diagrams correctly infers that the descent segments and the residential groupings are referred to by the same names. Furthermore, the same Ijaw terms categorize both of them although they are not identical units. Thus, the whole and each of the segments of Ebiebi's "family" are called *wari*, as are the divisions of the village. The former, however, are restricted in membership only by the fact of birth, whereas the latter—nonunilineal descent groups—are bounded by residence as well.[7] Depending on the context, *wari* means all the descendants of a living person, or of "a," or of "A," or ultimately of the village founder. Distinctions between *wari* are made on the basis of sex; a *dau wari* (father's family) refers to agnatic kinsmen and *nyinghi wari* (mother's family) to uterine kinsmen. In spacial terms *wari* means a house, or those family members living in the house, the subsection, or the section. *Dau wari* here means the residence of ego's father, implying some antiquity to the agnatic line residing in that section; *nyinghi wari* is more ambiguous because it refers to the residence of ego's mother before her

---

[7] For a discussion of nonunilineal descent groups, see Ward H. Goodenough, *Description and Comparison in Cultural Anthropology*, Chicago: Aldine Publishing Co., 1970.

marriage or to wherever her uterine kinsmen reside. An example of this terminology is shown by the following diagram:

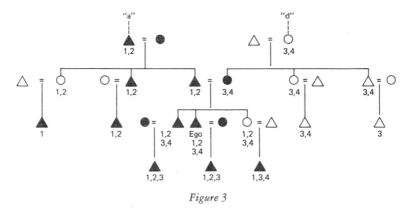

Figure 3

The darkened symbols are some of those kinsmen who might be found residing in subsection (*wari*) "a." Those numbered 1 are the descendants (*wari*) of person "a"; those also numbered 2 are ego's agnates (*dau wari*) called "a." On his mother's side ego is one of "d's" descendants (*wari*), 3; his uterine kinsmen (*nyinghi wari*) include those also numbered 4, which might be referred to as "d" or by the name of the residence of ego's mother's father.

Since marriage is prohibited to about third cousins, or as the Ijaw express it, between those still able to recall their exact genealogical connection, the bilateral ramifications of the kinship system should be apparent. Should ego start counting his father's mother's *wari* as well as his mother's father's, then the number of kinsmen and potential places of residence increases sharply. Although the range of places seems limited only by memory, experience and land tenure rights are considered by Ijaw to narrow the choices drastically. During childhood and early adulthood, individuals live in various places for reasons described above. The experience gained during this period influences an individual's choice of residence when he is ready to start his own household. Since the section is the focus of economic and political affairs, an Ijaw believes it is important to reside with those whom he likes and trusts.

Experience also imparts knowledge that is essential for a person to exercise his rights to property. Most of the farm land and fishing sites near Ebiama are held in the name of founders of sections and subsections. Usufruct and other considerations determine who exploits them. Unlike some other Ijaw villages where land is held by a corporate kin group and redistributed among its members each year, in Ebiama parcels of land are held indefinitely as long as they are farmed. In certain instances they also form a part of the inheritance for both men and women. This means, referring to Figure 3, that ego can receive land in "d" as well as in "a." Whether he does or not depends on his familiarity with the boundaries of his parents' land, his place of residence, and his line of descent to the *wari* holding title to the land. Should his mother fail to farm the land in "d" or to show him where the farms are located, ego might lose the opportunity to use them. The same is true for father's land, except residence in his father's section provides him access, in all likelihood, to its resources. Conversely, when a woman marries and resides elsewhere, she may lose her father's land after he dies. Whether she does or not depends on the goodwill of close relatives residing in her father's section. A woman usually remains in their favor as long as she maintains social contacts by visiting and contributing to funeral expenses of a section member. Nonetheless, the land can always be taken away from her because she has only a patrilineal claim to it.

Inheritance Matrilineally related kinsmen have the right to inherit from each other. For this reason the Ijaw judge uterine kinsmen to be their most important relatives. Both real property, such as money, houses, and slaves, and potential claims to serve a deity or to marry a widow are inherited by a man's full brother, or his sister's son, or his mother's brother, in that order of preference. Depending on the amount of the inheritance, everyone in ego's *nyinghi wari* (those numbered 4 in Figure 3) might share in his estate. Aside from land rights a woman inherits only the personal belongings of her mother and possibly the role of priestess to a deity after the incumbent, either her mother or another woman in her *nyinghi wari,* dies. With the benefits of inheritance also goes the responsibility for debts and funeral costs. Prior to British rule a man could pay his debts by pawning or selling into slavery a matrilineal relative. The relationship between members of a *nyinghi wari* is still expressed as the "right to sell one another," with the younger uterine kinsman being called *zi pẹrẹ tọbọu* (a child born as a gift to me).

Although inheritance rules seem to be highly specific, there is still room for exercising individual choice. Since European contact some men have attempted to change from matrilineal to patrilineal inheritance and thereby minimize the matrilineal privileges in land claims. Besides interpreting and wishing to imitate European customs in this regard, some Ijaw inherit from their fathers in one form of marriage to be described later. Furthermore, they argue that fathers bear the cost of raising sons and therefore should be allowed to reap any benefits should their sons die. The inverted order of inheritance indicates the small wealth of most men, and the hope that their sons will have more. Although the local courts resolve litigations in favor of traditional practice, a person with a "demonstrative personality" (*tọro krọ,* strong eye) may win his father's property because the matrilineal relatives wish to avoid a quarrel.

Types of Marriage and Associations The most prevalent type of marriage (93 percent of 212 marriages) in Ebiama is called a "small-dowry" marriage by English-speaking Ijaw. According to elders, no bridewealth at all was paid for a wife (*kala ikiya,* small friend) in pre-contact times. Subsequently, the amount became fixed at £12, of which £10 is paid to the bride's father and £2 to her mother and mother's brother. The husband acquires domestic, sexual, and some economic rights in his wife. Their children, however, are affiliated matrilineally.

The other type of marriage pertains to the remaining 7 percent of the married women. They are called "big-dowry" wives (*fẹ ẹrẹ,* purchased woman) because the bridewealth, though of unfixed amount, can be more than ten times the amount paid in small-dowry marriages. When slavery was still practiced, the *fẹ ẹrẹ* was thought to be virtually a slave status, and women born in the Ebiama area will not agree to become this type of wife. A big-dowry wife must be sought, therefore, on the mainland or from among the Ijaw living in the northern part of the Delta.

The definition of "slave" in this case depends on a consideration of rights transferred to the husband on payment of bridewealth and not on any kind of inferior treatment accorded the *fẹ ẹrẹ*. In a big-dowry marriage the husband acquires domestic, sexual, and all economic rights in his wife. A man gains prestige by marrying in this way, but most importantly, he obtains all rights to his children, and they are members of his own descent groups. His wife similarly affiliates with his kinsmen and severs all ties with her own. She must receive her farm land from her husband, and their children will inherit from him rather than from her brother. There is no stigma to having been born of a big-dowry marriage. These children often have an advantage because they must be provided for by their father and his kinsmen who believe they are a source of pride. Big-dowry wives are valuable, then, because their children must add to the size of their husbands' residential groups. The possibility of children going to reside with their maternal kinsmen has been eliminated.

Cutting across the ties of marriage and consanguinity that extend throughout the community and beyond to the surrounding villages are several groups organized on criteria other than genealogy. Cult-houses and the Christian churches draw their membership on the basis of interest and need, though only matrilineal descendants are "chosen" by deities to replace deceased cult leaders. Age-groups (*zi ogbo*) are another example of associational organizations. They consist of males and females born within a few months of each other. Members of the same *zi ogbo* know each other from childhood but are not identified by any particular name. Although they have a joking relationship and may insult one another freely, the members meet together rarely, usually only if one of them kills a large animal and presents one of its legs for a feast. The age-groups have an indirect importance in political affairs by establishing a chronological ordering of the population. Relative age, as we will see, is a significant factor in the patterning of authority.

THE VALUE OF WORK

The Niger Delta has two principal seasons. A comparatively dry period lasts from November to March. During the other months it rains, except for a brief hiatus in July and August. The rains result in an annual rise in the waters of the Niger. Unlike villages located on main rivers, Ebiama is rarely flooded even though its river bank rises less than twenty feet above the water during the dry season. Nearby lower land is completely inundated each year.

Much of the dense rain forest surrounding Ebiama is swampy throughout the year. Wild raffia palms are found here in great quantities and are tapped for their sap, called palm wine. In the drier portions grow palm oil trees and a variety of other trees suitable for manufacturing dugout canoes and building houses. Areas of the drier forest are cleared for cultivation, but after a year or two these farms must be left to lie fallow for seven to ten years. Farms along the river banks are more highly valued since flooding allows them to be cultivated year after year.

Subsequent to trading with Nembe middlemen for European goods, Ebiama men sold their palm oil and palm kernels to a station on the Nun River opened by the Royal Niger Company about 1895 and continued in operation under the aegis of the United Africa Company. For their produce the Ebiama men first received cases of gin which served as a medium of exchange until English currency was introduced early in the twentieth century. The forest provides raw materials for the fabrication of innumerable items in everyday use, ranging from bamboo and raffia for fishing baskets to palm leaves for thatch; but for as long as anyone in Ebiama can recall, the village has always depended on outside sources for woven cloth and for objects made of metal. They purchase metal cooking utensils, cloths, salt, clocks, cement, corrugated iron sheets for roofing, and occasionally canned foods on trading trips to mainland cities or from the United Africa Company. In addition, Igbo blacksmiths, one of whom settled in a nearby village, travel with their wares in the Delta providing a variety of tools, fishing hooks, and flintlock guns for hunting.

The production of palm oil was the major occupation of most of the men at Ebiama. Though only a few actually continue with the operation, they still recognize it as the traditional labor of men and one which every Ijaw male should learn before turning to other work. Oil palms generally grow wild and the ripened bunches of fruit may be cut by the first person to find them. The season for collecting palm fruits lasts from December to June, ending with the first heavy rains. After a man has gathered a large number of bunches, he is helped by his wives and children to remove the berries from the stalks. Formerly the men of the community joined in cooperative work groups for the most arduous phase of extraction. When one member of a group was ready, he cooked the berries and called the others to come to mash them with their feet to separate the pulp from the nut core in large, communally owned troughs. Those members failing without good reason to participate, or who came late, were fined by their colleagues, but the strongest motivation for cooperating was the desire to have others reciprocate.[8] In the final stage the oil producers with the help of their wives only placed the mash in canoes filled with water. As the oil separated from the pulp and floated to the top, it was skimmed off and boiled to remove the impurities. The palm nuts were cracked to remove the shell and also sold.

Prior to 1940 only a few men tapped raffia palms to provide palm wine free of charge for social and ritual occasions. In the 1930s a method of distilling "illicit gin" from palm wine was introduced,[9] though it is not remembered precisely by whom. By 1958 most men had become gin distillers. The stills are built in swamp-

---

[8] The few men still collecting palm fruit usually perform this phase of the work by themselves.

[9] English-speaking Ijaw refer to this colorless, potent drink as "illicit gin" because, besides being illegal to produce, it resembles the gin introduced earlier in the century by European traders.

land near the trees, since about eleven gallons of palm wine will yield only one gallon of gin. Whenever the exhaustion of available trees requires a new location, each man rebuilds his still wherever he finds ripe trees, as long as he is not too close to any other distillery. Because a man must spend most of his time collecting the raw juice, his wife usually accompanies him and tends to the process of boiling the palm wine. The gin is sold in the village by the bottle or in bulk to traders who smuggle it into Calabar.

Other endeavors, followed as specialties by only a few men in the village, or as part-time work, include fishing, carving canoes, cutting and hauling timber, weaving thatch, and trading. Only one man residing in Ebiama depends on fishing for his livelihood, selling his catch for cash or occasionally bartering it for farm produce. All men know how to fish, and many of them at some time during their lives travel for this purpose to the Kalabari area or to Calabar and remain there for months or several years at a time.

Canoes are, of course, a basic item among the possessions of an Ijaw, and most men can make them well enough to meet the needs of their own families. Men particularly proficient at carving canoes occasionally make them for sale. An element of cooperative labor is found in this work, especially at the time a large canoe is fired to spread its sides. Unlike the manufacture of palm oil, instead of reciprocity being important, helpers are "thanked" with a drink of palm wine or gin.

Hunters, using flintlock guns and traps, occasionally bring in a monkey, antelope, or a wild pig. A large kill not only allows distribution to certain kinsmen and to age-mates as gifts, but also provides a surplus for sale. For the most part, however, the game caught is small and hunters obtain scarcely enough meat for the needs of their own households.

Aside from trading, which will be discussed below, the remaining tasks performed by men include weaving thatch mats for roofing, making fishing equipment and household implements, and cutting timber on contract with timber buyers from the mainland. These provide additional income but are of minor consideration in the day-to-day economy.

A woman's principal occupation is to maintain her household by providing food from farming and fishing, by cooking, and by caring for her children. She may supplement this work by assisting her husband in distilling gin or processing oil. Women begin the farming season in November or early December after the flood waters subside. They clear two or three plots of land, averaging 250 ft by 75 ft each, and plant the staples of the Ijaw diet: cassava, plantain, cocoyams, sugar cane, and pepper. Except for plantain, which is generally planted on high ground, crops must be harvested before the Niger again begins to rise in August and September. A woman usually weeds her farms twice during the growing season, sometimes with the help of her older unmarried children or of other women with whom she reciprocates. Men cut down the large trees to clear new fields for their wives, but they have no further responsibilities.

Few women have the land, energy, and good fortune to produce more food during a given season than is needed for household consumption. More often vegetable and fruit staples must be supplemented with purchases of yams and "gari," specially prepared cassava meal, from markets in the northern part of the Delta. Nonetheless, should a woman fear her root crops will rot or her plantain ripen before she can use them, she will sell them and use the money to buy food later. This condition pertains to crops she grows on her own farms, that is, those obtained from her mother or father. If she sells plantain from plots belonging to her husband, she gives him the proceeds.

During the rainy season, and during lulls in the farming cycle, women occupy themselves by weaving fishing traps for use in the river or forest ponds. Fishing in the river is essentially an individual activity, though a woman might ask her daughter to paddle while she herself baits and throws out the hooks. Fishing in ponds is always done in groups. Several women enter a shallow pool together to drive the fish to one side where they can easily be killed, but each participant claims only those fish she herself catches. As with agricultural staples, there are rarely enough fish in excess of household demands to warrant selling any of the catch, especially since fish is a prized item in the daily diet. If, as happens occasionally during the floods, there is a surplus, the women dry and sell the fish to traders keeping the proceeds for themselves.

Within the memory of the oldest inhabitants, villagers once produced enough food to sustain themselves and bartered only occasionally for fish and salt from nearby villages in the mangrove area. Markets existed in distant Ijaw communities, and trading was undertaken by none but the most courageous men. Whatever the reasons for the increased need—a larger population or a change in taste—families in Ebiama since the imposition of British control frequently require more than they can grow, and eat foods, such as gari and yams, they never produced. Yet, despite the need to import many items, few Ijaw in Ebiama are traders. Some men own small shops in the village and sell manufactured items they have purchased at the United Africa Company station or on long trips to the urban centers of Port Harcourt or Onitsha; others purchase food at the markets in the Delta, all several days away by canoe, for sale at Ebiama and nearby villages. A few women also buy food to sell, but trading is a relatively new occupation for them.

Although a woman can make a profit from her two principal endeavors, farming and fishing, her goal is primarily to produce food for the household. When she has the time, a woman earns a little money by weaving baskets and mats, helping other women farm, paddling for traders, and mudding walls of houses. By contrast, virtually all the labor of men results in a cash return with which they can assist their wives in purchasing food or in buying items that must be imported. Men also use the money they earn for taxes, contributions to village undertakings, school fees for their children, bridewealth, and funeral obligations. Items of prestige—corrugated iron roofing and big-dowry wives—are particularly expensive. Women require lesser amounts of money than men for village and funeral contributions, but if they are able they provide the school fees for their children and may help pay their husbands' taxes.

The motivation for working cannot be said to lie wholly in meeting financial obligations or household needs, even though these are the most obvious reasons. Also of importance is the emphatic value placed on independence which is defined in the economic sphere of activities as the ability to perform arduous tasks, to maintain oneself, and to carry on an occupation without having to depend on others for help. These attitudes are apparent in the behavior and statements of old men and women who continue to work for almost as long as they can walk, and, unless infirm, refuse to become dependent on their children. The Ijaw concern with productive labor, together with the probability that there was little or no economic surplus in aboriginal times, helps to account for the absence of full-time specialists in religious and political offices and in other spheres of activity.

Women affirm the desirability of working independently less emphatically than do men, as is evident from their occasional cooperative farming and fishing excursions. Still, when women form a group to accomplish some task, each works individually. In farming, for example, a field is divided into sections and each woman clears her allotted share. On joint work projects in which both men and women take part, whether it be clearing a forest path or building a house for a schoolteacher, the work is divided equally among the participants. The Ijaw believe this individual approach to work is the best way to avoid conflicts. Supposedly with equal assignments there can be no dispute as to whether a particular person does more or less than his share of a given task.

AUTHORITY AND POLITICS

All decisions to act as a group are based on the consensus of the relevant part of the community, whether the smallest subsection or the village as a whole. Decisions are shaped by leaders who, by definition, are men able to speak eloquently and sway the majority toward their opinions. A person with leadership abilities can sometimes be referred to as an *alotu,* the term applied both to a war leader of the past and to a champion wrestler, but ordinarily his position is implicit. Leaders exist to the extent that their authority results in action.

Age has a bearing on authority because Ijaw believe wisdom should accompany it. Before schooling and a knowledge of English became important assets for understanding governmental matters, young men probably had a minor influence on debates. An elderly man, on the other hand, automatically receives the rituals of respect from those younger than himself, but he too must demonstrate his intellectual abilities in order to exert a strong influence.

Prior to British administration there was neither a hierarchical political structure nor titled positions. Subsequently, the colonial regime superimposed political innovations upon the traditional units of kinship and residence. The *ibe,* the basis for clans, became increasingly important units in governmental organization. Since about 1945 a council of elected representatives from each village in Opuama meets once or twice during the year to discuss ways of "improving" the clan. On several occasions the council voted to abrogate traditional customs thought to be repugnant to present-day standards of conduct. The council also decided an Opuama Clan market should be built to encourage trade. These decisions are advisory, however, and their implementation depends on the support of the people in each village. In 1958 the Eastern Regional Government ordered each clan to elect a clan chief or "king" (*ibenanawei,* owner of the *ibe*) as its representative in a hierarchy of positions leading to a newly created House of Chiefs. Despite lack of precedence and information on the duties and rights for such a post, a clan chief was finally elected for a life term.

Similar to the *ibe,* the village as a whole acquired political functions only after the advent of British rule. Villagers were required to act together on community projects that entailed organizing cooperative work programs to construct a school-house and to clear paths. About 1930[10] a man was elected to the lifetime office of village head (*amananawei* or *amayanabo,* owner of the village). Apparently his duties were so few and his power so minimized by the individualistic pattern of authority that after his death in the early 1940s another *amananawei* was not chosen until 1958. The Eastern Regional Government requested that the election take place, but as in the case both of the first village head and of the clan chief, his duties were ill-defined and his powers negligible.

Even with these innovations the most significant political aggregates continue to be the sections and subsections. Prior to the Pax Brittanica the section, aided by the eponymous ancestor's descendants living in other parts of the village or nearby communities, was the major segment to participate in feuds with com-parable units of other villages. These armed conflicts resulted from failure of a member of one section to pay a debt to the member of another or from a murder or accidental killing involving members of two different sections. Blood feuds were evidence of the greater loyalty due co-residential kinsmen than others, for a man would join them in battle against another section containing close relatives. Indi-viduals in this predicament, however, would try to mediate the argument before it came to the point of fighting. Even in a dispute with her parents' section, a woman was expected to support her husband. Covenants to settle feuds were made in the names of sections.

The section remains important in times of peace. The oldest man, on the advice of the houschold heads, can call a meeting of all the men in the section for any number of reasons. For example, the group meets to settle an argument between members, to set a date to fish a lake belonging to the section, or to arrange for enter-taining guests at the time of a funeral. Land held in the name of the section founder also requires the attention of the members should there be a boundary dispute with another section. The latter problem usually requires that the women working the disputed land attend the meeting, but otherwise, females are excluded from consultations.

Subsection meetings are called for many of the same reasons that bring the mem-bers of a section together. If rights to land or a pond are held in the name of the founder of the subsection, household heads meet to discuss boundary disputes or to set dates for fishing. One topic in the past never discussed by a subsection alone was the possibility of engaging in a feud; this was reserved for meetings of the whole section.

Although decisions are reached by mutual consent, the political structure has few

---

[10] Ijaw estimate the date was 1920, but the District Officer's report of 1931 makes no mention of a village head or "warrant chief." Furthermore, although the Native Authority system began to be applied in Southern Nigeria in 1916, legislation in the East "cannot be said to have been effective until 1934" (L. Gray Cowan, *Local Government in West Africa,* New York: Columbia University Press, 1958, p. 18).

built-in mechanisms for forcing members to participate in village, section, or sub-section agreements. Should a person fail to cooperate, fellow members of whichever unit is involved would insult and argue with him and, more threateningly, they would refuse to aid him should he require their assistance at another time. After the British instituted Native Courts, an individual could be fined for refusing to work on certain types of community projects.

The Native Court for Ebiama is located at Rotoma, approximately three hours away by canoe. The district officer selects the judges from the villages in the area and their decisions on minor offenses are supposed to be in accordance with traditional customs. The inconvenience and cost of going to court induces most disputants to try and settle their problems by traditional methods of media-tion. When an individual inadvertently destroys or damages another person's property, one form of mediation occurs by sending a mediator to beg forgiveness. Intermediaries are generally successful, since an admission of guilt by the offender all but obligates the offended party to excuse the act without requesting compen-sation, even for valuable property. Should a man dismiss the mediator and insist on retribution, particularly for a personal injury, he faces similar treatment at a later time if he tries to settle a grievance. Another alternative, especially pertinent when individuals threaten to physically harm each other, is for a third party to take the initiative in settling a dispute by offering to mediate.

Another form of mediation takes place in arbitrations. The disputants call in a respected third party to judge their case. On the basis of evidence presented by witnesses, he determines who is guilty and what his fine should be. The judge has no power to enforce his decision. Should the loser ignore him, the penalty may be left to deities called upon to redress the wrong or, in the past, the result could have been a blood feud. Before serious crimes, principally murder and theft, came under the jurisdiction of the Government, offenders were killed or sold away by their own kinsmen. In the case of sorcery, as with other offenses, the Ijaw believe the fear of the power of deities remains the ultimate way to protect individuals and to deter antisocial acts.

The Ijaw emphasis on individualism finds its most expressive medium in political affairs. Their world view tempers this expression by dictating that many social norms are prescribed by non-human forces, that is, they are outside the sphere of human control.

FATE AND ITS FULFILLMENT

The Ijaw believe Wǫnyinghi (our mother) resides in the sky, far distant from the mundane affairs of daily living. Yet, she created everything and is the final arbiter of their fate. Few Ijaw villages have organized cult groups dedicated specifi-cally to her worship. In Ebiama the entire village participated in annual festivals for Wǫnyinghi until her priestess died in 1950. Since then Wǫnyinghi has not chosen a replacement for the priestess, organized ceremonies for her have stopped, and her shrine has all but collapsed from lack of care.

Ijaw mention Wǫnyinghi most frequently in discussing man's fate and the reasons for death. Every human being has a "soul" (*tẹmẹ*) that appears before Wọnyinghi prior to entering the womb of a woman. The *tẹmẹ* informs the Creator as to the nature of his future life—whether he will be rich or poor, healthy or ill, prolific or barren, and when he will die. Ijaw explain why a *tẹmẹ* chooses to request ill-fortune by referring to the naiveté to be expected of an unborn *tẹmẹ*.

The consultation between a *tẹmẹ* and Wọnyinghi is referred to as "the agreement." The agreement can sometimes be amended by a diviner performing rituals to request Wọnyinghi to allow a petitioner who leads a life of adversity to have a favorable future. Considering the moral value placed on work, it is not surprising that the Creator is never asked for money or material goods per se; rather, she is asked to make the work of the propitiant productive so that he will prosper. ·

The exact time at which a person has agreed to die is learned *ex post facto,* after his death, when his *tẹmẹ* is consulted concerning the reasons for his death. Except for children who die before their first teeth erupt and are, therefore, buried without ceremony, these facts are revealed by means of an *obẹbẹ* (ladder), a short three-rung ladder, or of a coffin. Either one is constructed immediately after the death is announced. Four men lift the *obẹbẹ* or coffin while a fifth man asks questions. The *tẹmẹ* of the deceased answers by moving the four men forward to indicate "yes" or backward to say "no." Invariably the *tẹmẹ* responds positively to the question of whether one of the causes of death was due to its agreement with Wọnyinghi.

After the funeral the *tẹmẹ* enters a new foetus, perhaps as part of its initial agreement, or resides permanently in a village of the dead. Sometimes ancestors (*duwoiyou*) return as ghosts (also called *duwoiyou*) to kill or injure anyone encountering them. Ordinarily the ancestors are thought to remain in their own villages and to protect their living kinsmen, causing illness or death only if they are offended for some reason. When the latter occurs, the living must propitiate them with food and drink. There are no shrines or images representing the *duwoiyou,* and, except for mollifying offended ancestors, people serve them only by pouring a few drops of liquid on the ground before taking a drink.

The most important ancestors are the *opuduwoiyou* (great dead people). They include the three sons of Ebiebi and men and women who were great-grandparents during their lifetimes. They have their own village of the dead and "eat together." Should humans behave immorally in certain ways, for example, by a big-dowry wife committing adultery, by a woman assuming the top position during sexual intercourse, or by kinsmen having incestuous relations, the *opuduwoiyou* cause the offenders to be ill or barren until they are propitiated.

Although Wọnyinghi and the ancestors play significant roles in the Ijaw world view, they are somewhat removed from many pressing problems felt by individuals. To deal with severe illness, barrenness, sorcery, theft, and bad luck, the Ijaw turn for help to the nearby local deities (*orumọ*). They reside in the forest and in the rivers, or, by their own volition, in human communities. An *oru* discloses its presence by making a person ill or by coming to him in a dream. These events are interpreted by a diviner to be signs that an *oru* wishes to be served. The diviner instructs the man or woman so chosen on what type of wooden figure should be carved to represent it and the food taboos or other prohibitions to be followed. The *oru* in return is supposed to protect its devotee from misfortune and to grant requests for more children, a healthy life, and other benefits.

If an *oru* demonstrates more than average power, not only in protecting and providing for its attendants but in causing people from Ebiama and nearby villages to come to ask favors of it as well, a cult-organization forms. The initial propitiant becomes the priest. Other positions in the cult are filled by people whose illnesses or dreams are diagnosed by a diviner or the *oru* priest to be caused by the *oru*. Participation cuts across kinship lines, and individuals can belong to more than one cult.

The number of participants in any one cult varies with the reputation of the *oru*. Of the three active cult-houses in Ebiama, the one best known for its power (*biyẹ krọ,* strength over anything) claims the presence of at least forty attendants, including men and women, during important rituals. The *oru* with the smallest reputation may have only seven or eight. Strength, measured explicitly by the number of people coming to serve the *oru,* means wealth since each visitor making a request must offer the *oru* money as well as food and drink. The affluence of the *oru* is reflected in its house, the wealthiest one in Ebiama having a concrete floor and corrugated iron roof. Shrines of less powerful deities are built of mud and thatch.

Whether *orumọ* grow stronger, spreading their reputations throughout the Delta, or become virtually extinct, depends largely on their success as agents of social control. A few of the *orumọ* have become famous for their ability to apprehend thieves and sorcerers. Their method is not to slay the offender, but rather one of his close relatives. The guilty party is still able to come to the *oru* to confess and make restitution. If a thief confesses and returns stolen property before anyone in his family dies, he pays a large fee, usually prescribed in the initial petition, to the *oru*. Should a death occur, the expense is greater. His relatives feel compelled to assist him in raising the amount of his fine, since they are the ones in danger until the invocation is repealed.

In other circumstances, when opponents in a dispute present contradictory evidence, or adultery is suspected but denied by the wife, and there are no witnesses to support either side, an oath can be sworn by both parties asking an *oru* to punish the guilty party. The final outcome of these disputes is not known until one of the principals or one of his kinsmen dies.

The possibility that *orumọ* have already been asked for protection makes them powerful deterrents to antisocial behavior. To indicate that an *oru* has been summoned, some sign, usually in the form of a shaft of grass tied in a special way, is left in full view on the protected property, whether it be on a farm or a pile of firewood. Deities are also given offerings and requested to attack anyone attempting to work evil on the devotee.

The descriptive term for a powerful *oru* is also applied to a type of human personality. A person or *oru* with *biyẹ krọ* is strong and carries out his intentions without talking about them; someone who talks forcefully and threateningly but does not necessarily act is *tọro krọ*. As in humans, the Ijaw accept the manifestation of personality traits in deities without being particularly concerned about their source. Asked for an explanation of the derivation of power, the elders simply say the *orumọ*, like men, are created by Wọnyinghi and gain their attributes from her. Ijaw explain that the power of an *oru* ebbs or grows stronger for various reasons: the will of the Creator, the departure of the *oru* from the village, the death of its priest and failure to select a new one, or its dehabilitation by a person bringing poison (*sei diri*, bad medicine) into the cult-house. An *oru* reveals its weakness by its apparent inabilty to protect or provide good fortune for its followers. As a consequence the figurine will be discarded or ignored, perhaps until the deity "returns" at some future time and is resuscitated by making its presence known through the diagnosis of a diviner.

Closely associated with the *orumọ* are the *owumọ*. These are carved masks, usually in the form of fish, that are worn on the top of the head. They are said to be copies of masks worn by the deities as they dance on sandbars. They can also be *orumọ*, distinguishable by reference to their place of origin and type of figurine. *Orumọ*, in other words, come from the forest or the rivers, but *owumọ* only from the water. When an *owu* is a carved figurine into which a deity has entered, all the above discussion pertaining to the *orumọ* applies to the *owumọ* as well. Furthermore, if the *owu* has been invoked and has killed someone, the guilty party, in addition to usual costs, must also pay for an expensive ceremonial dance employing the masks.

Some masks are carved for exclusively secular reasons. In this case an *owu* is not an *oru*. Two or three secular *owu* masks are worn by men at the funeral of an important man—a person who has surviving grandchilden or great-grandchildren —or in recent times for the celebration of Christmas. Cloths are hung from the masks to hide the dancers' faces. They carry small machetes and occasionally chase the onlookers, threatening to cut them. Unlike the religious *owu* dances, the identities of the dancers are known and a masquerader would be careful not to inflict a wound for fear of retaliation.

Although the sacred and secular dances are similar in many ways, a secular *owu* is not worshipped nor does it display any power by making people ill. Furthermore, in a sacred *owu* dance the masquaraders are considered to be the deities themselves. The dancers are secretly dressed and exercise the privilege of slashing any member of the audience they can catch.

The Ijaw see no subdivision of *orumọ* inhabiting the forest comparable to that of *oru-owu* from the rivers. Instead they posit several other types of beings, called "forest people" (*bouyou*) and "forest things" (*bouyei*), to populate the land. Whenever an offering of food is made in the cult-houses, usually a small portion is put aside to placate inhabitants of the forest who might happen to be on the scene. Human beings must avoid direct contact with forest beings on pain of illness and possible death, though sometimes one realizes he has had contact only after a misfortune occurs and a diviner is consulted.

The two diviners (*buroyou*) in Ebiama are women, but men are known to have acted in this capacity in earlier generations. Their importance should by this point be self-evident, since their diagnostic abilities enable them continually to play the pivotal position between the observable and the unknown. They attempt to answer the imponderable questions of daily life: why one person is ill while another is healthy, one injured in an accident while another is safe, one woman barren while another has many children. Diviners have the means of determining a man's fate by changing his agreement with Wǫnyinghi, but this is only one of many reasons why a man may be suffering misfortune. A sorcerer (*diriguǫkęmę*, worker of bad medicine), that is, one who harms others secretly and intentionally by direct poisoning or magical means, may also be at work; an *oru* may require propitiation; or, an ancestor may demand attention. The diviners, with knowledge derived from dreams and from understanding the language of birds and animals, and with power from their personal *orumǫ* to read divining paraphernalia and to apply herbal remedies, direct an individual towards the method of defeating an adversary or soothing the appropriate spiritual powers.

Except for the Christians, who express total disbelief in diviners, most of the Ijaw in Ebiama consider the role of diviner to be undeniably important, but they often question the ability of particular diviners. The aphorism, "a prophet is not without honor, save in his own country, and in his own house," applies to the diviner. Villagers believe a *burokęmę* living in a distant place usually has more power than one in their own community. Presumably there is less likelihood of a foreign diviner "cheating" by interpreting the problem of the applicant in the light of gossip or facts commonly known in his home village. Another explanation for this phenomenon may be that successful interpretations and cures by diviners are communicated widely, while their failures are more obvious to people in the immediate vicinity.

Whereas a diviner tries to help the community, sorcerers attempt to do evil. The *diriguǫyou* are thought to be women usually; and big-dowry wives are particularly suspect since they come from other areas. The Ijaw presume an individual becomes a sorcerer by his own volition, though the specific benefits derived from this choice are unclear. The vampire (*foun*, one who flies) is a recent innovation in the belief system in Ebiama, since none are remembered to have been present prior to 1950. A *foun* has wings and flies in the night, sucks blood to kill its victim and, unlike the *diriguǫkęmę,* can induce others to become *founyou* without their knowledge by giving them human blood to drink. Ijaw fear the power of *diriguǫyou* and *founyou,* and frequently ask *orumǫ* for protection. In addition etiquette requires the person serving a drink to taste it to indicate no poison has been added. Adults are cautious to eat only with friends or kinsmen, and children are taught to refuse food proffered by strangers.

In sum, Ebiama is a slowly changing community where social relations are still based on kinship ties and ultimately regulated by religious sanctions. The absence of a political hierarchy or ascribed statuses, beyond age and sex, combines with values on individual choice to give the Ijaw the appearance of being equalitarian in their ideology and flexible in their organization. We turn now to the way individuals come to learn and thereby to perpetuate these social and cultural characteristics.

3 / The prenatal setting

THE PREDISPOSITIONS OF PROSPECTIVE PARENTS, shaped by the cultural and social context described in the previous chapter and by an awareness that less than 50 percent of the children born will survive their first year of life, must be seen as affecting the desire to conceive and the pattern of child rearing. Ijaw want to have as many children as possible. Ideally a woman should bear two children every three years. This goal stems from several factors, but to adult Ijaw in Ebiama reproduction is a value *sui generis*. Furthermore, the desire for children affects the stability of marriage and results in a host of measures for influencing the favorable course of pregnancy and parturition. Barrenness or sterility creates an inferior status for a person during his lifetime and even after death. Both parents are believed to contribute equally to the conception of a child. Procreation has particular significance to the Ijaw because they do not practice adoption; the functions of biological and social paternity are inseparable.

The importance of childbearing is accurately reflected in the several special terms used to describe the physical development and marital status of a female. A girl is referred to as *yeibiniteiyara* after she has agreed to marry. Terms of direct address include *ayoroba*, newly wed; *kala amata*, married but as yet without child; and *ziyara*, a woman who has just given birth. The term of reference for a barren woman or one past menopause is *zifa*. By contrast there is a paucity of Ijaw terms for male statuses at any period of the life cycle. A man can be insulted, however, by being reminded that he has had no children.

REASONS FOR WANTING CHILDREN

The clearest expression of the principal function of marriage for Ijaw is found in their frequent reference to infertility as the prime cause for divorce. A woman failing to conceive within a reasonable time after marriage has sufficient grounds to divorce her husband, and will be encouraged to do so by her kinsmen. In this situation a man would not wish to divorce since he can marry other women to bear his children.

Aside from the problem of divorce, the desire to enlarge the family (*wari*) receives impetus from a number of specific benefits. When feuds were fought, a large family was essential to waging a successful campaign, and even though blood feuds have ceased, the potential for physical aggression remains constant. Having many children acts as a deterrent to those who might otherwise provoke a fight. In everyday affairs unmarried children provide assistance in household and productive tasks. Finally, old age is an important criterion for demanding and receiving respect, but an elderly person without descendants has little prestige. A barren woman, in particular, is continually open to insults and gossip as to the causes of her misfortune.

Parents deny a strong preference for either sons or daughters, but men tend to want sons. A father expects his sons to build their houses nearby, help him when he is ill, protect him from abuse, and give him a proper funeral. Daughters, on the other hand, move away at marriage to join their husbands. Their practical advantage to a father is in providing him with a large share of their bridewealth. Yet, few men give this as a primary reason for wanting daughters as well as sons. Since Ijaw believe the desire for children is natural, rationalizations are needed only for the inquiring anthropologist.

Women give the same reasons as men for preferring sons, adding that daughters-in-law can aid them, and that their sons' children will be close by. Some small-dowry wives, however, say they prefer to have daughters because the children of daughters will be of their own matri-family (*nyinghi wari*). In addition, female children are wanted because they have special roles during funerals. As one mother pointed out, "It is only my daughter or a woman in my family who will cover my genitals with a cloth when I die, not my son."

The respect and prestige accorded a man or woman who both reaches old age and has a large family comes to a symbolic climax at the time of his death. For a person with great-grandchildren an elaborate coffin is built, special ritual and *owu* dances are performed, and all-night wakes are held. The funeral observances may last for a year after the burial. During this time guests from villages a great distance away come to offer their respects. The funeral for a grandparent is only slightly less elaborate. These funerals, the most resplendent events in the experience of those living in Ebiama, celebrate the highest achievements of life: old age and productive parenthood.

When a younger person, with children but not grandchildren, dies, he is buried in a simple coffin without ceremony. Grief can be intensely expressed, particularly if either of the parents of the deceased is still alive, in contrast to the formalized wailing for an elderly person. Three days after the burial of a man, or four days for a woman, a meal is served to encourage the *tẹmẹ* of the deceased to leave for the villages of the dead. From now on he will "eat" with other people of his own ranking: great-grandparents join with the founding ancestors of the village, grandparents eat together, and parents with only one generation of descendants gather with others of their category.

In sharp contrast, those dying without progeny are buried in a mat, as a child is buried, and no food is offered them following the burial. To have a burial of this sort is considered a tragedy. Without descendants a person must face oblivion since an ancestor can expect to be remembered and responded to only by his children and their children.

CONCEPTION

The pervasive desire for offspring generates a great concern over conception and pregnancy. Girls are expected to remain virgins until they agree to marry and have their menarche. Once these events have occurred they can discreetly begin to have sexual intercourse with their intended husbands. Although the Ijaw know that copulation is a prerequisite for conception, they attempt various means to aid conception. Since women are thought to be most fertile just after their menses, a man polygynously married will break his regular cycle of visits to his wives to have intercourse with a new wife at this time, or, for that matter, with any one of his wives who has not conceived for some time. In addition, a husband may ask a young girl, eleven or twelve years old, to assist his bride for the first few weeks after marriage. This girl will sleep in the same room, and perhaps in the same bed, with the couple. Only a few elders say her presence on the bed is related to the bride's conceiving quickly, but Ijaw generally agree that any contact with young children helps a woman become pregnant.

The importance of touching children, particularly carrying babies on the back, suggests a kind of imitative magic, but it also relates logically to a more general set of beliefs which attributes special powers to children.[1] For example, on one occasion, a woman wishing to become pregnant gave sugar cane to four- and five-year-old children. She requested a child in return, and they readily chorused their agreement. Although she seemed to be joking, the woman later professed that she felt the children's response might help her. Other women believe that when a youngster asks his mother for a baby to carry, the mother may become pregnant that month.

When a frog with a very smooth skin, like that of a baby, enters a house, some Ijaw also interpret this as a sign the woman in the household will soon conceive. In the past, according to an elderly informant, a woman wanting children would try to find a frog of this kind, would wash and tie it to her back, and call the frog her child. A current, popular method for inducing pregnancy is to visit a masseur (*iyọloli*), referred to as a "presser" by English-speaking Ijaw, to have the womb put into proper position by violent kneeding and twisting. In addition, non-Christian couples always ask the *orumọ* "to bring" children and promise food and drink in return. As a consequence, the majority of offerings made in the cult-houses are in support of petitions for children, or to protect mother and child during pregnancy and parturition. These requests carry promises of further offerings if the prayers are granted.

If massaging and imitative actions fail, sterility may be attributed to other types of causes. In the agreement between the *tẹmẹ* of a woman and Wọnyinghi, the *tẹmẹ* may have asked that the woman remain barren all her life, or not become pregnant again after delivering one child. A second cause could be an *oru*'s displeasure at some offense. Thirdly, sorcerers are believed to incur barrenness by

---

[1] See page 48.

employing "bad medicine" or by nailing an undefinable "something to a tree that is believed to "pin" the victim so she cannot conceive. A rope can also be placed across the road and the name of the victim spoken, thereby "tying" her and preventing conception. A sorcerer can dig up and use the body of an infant to induce subsequent barrenness for its mother. This possibility explains why children dying in infancy were thrown into the river to dispose of them, but under British law the practice was outlawed. A final cause may be an offended ancestor or the ancient ancestors of the village who wish to signify their displeasure. In all these cases a diviner is sought to prescribe the medicines and, in many instances, perform the rituals necessary to rectify the transgression or counteract the evil.

If a woman still fails to conceive, a common solution, as already mentioned, is divorce. The problem of whether the husband or wife is at fault, however, can sometimes be a complicated one. For example, both the man and woman may have children by previous marriages. In such cases, Ijaw believe some men and women simply do not mix well.

Despite the consequences of barrenness and despite the desire for children, in certain situations women reportedly consider or induce abortion by using herbs or laundry bluing. There is little factual information, however, about the actual frequency of abortion. Schoolgirls are said to try to cause abortions when they conceive before a marriage agreement is reached, but from their reputation for having to leave school abruptly, it would seem they are not very successful. Women conceiving too soon after a recent delivery sometimes try to abort. Also, the mother of twins might induce abortion during her next pregnancy to free herself quickly of restrictions following a twin delivery.

If abortion is not attempted or is unsuccessful, an unmarried girl must always announce the father of her child. A promiscuous girl names the first man with whom she had intercourse after her last menses. Sometimes disputes arise because a man wants to be chosen as the father, particularly in the case of a woman divorcing and moving directly to another man, but the testimony of the woman is usually final.

PREGNANCY AND PARTURITION

Pregnancy is first recognized by the cessation of menses, the onset of weak periods while working, and is finally diagnosed by "pressers" after they have massaged the stomach of the woman. The period of pregnancy does not greatly alter routine unless a woman already has a small infant who must now be weaned. She continues to farm and fish up to the time of delivery. An expectant mother prepares herself during pregnancy for postpartum inactivity by gathering and storing food, and usually she weaves a new mat to lie on during her recovery. During the period of pregnancy women report that they have peculiarities in their tastes and smells. Some dislike cassava or plantain, while others crave oranges, or the taste and odor of dried mud. Sexual intercourse is permitted until delivery, but some men are dissuaded by the movements of the foetus after pregnancy is well advanced. A husband treats his pregnant wife with some deference, generally described by women as being "kind." Should she be in pain, he will stay up at night to comfort her, and if there is no one else to help, he might cook for her or perhaps heat water for her bath.

The few restrictions placed on the movements of a pregnant woman pertain to the precautions she must take to avoid certain powers that may harm the foetus. Portions of the forest are prohibited to her because of the *orumọ* residing there. A path between Ebiama and a nearby village was forbidden to pregnant women in earlier days because it passed through "bad bush," where women dying in pregnancy are buried, but this prohibition was ignored after a pregnant woman used the path and still experienced a successful delivery. Precautions also result from the belief that association produces likeness in the unborn child. A pregnant woman, for example, should never pick up a lame animal, or look at an ugly person. Events beyond the village are also thought to influence the foetus, such as the Okrika-Kalabari War in 1950, which the Ijaw believe caused many children born that year to have bodily and temperamental defects.

Preparations for parturition center mainly on medical treatment. A woman can obtain herbal mixtures from a midwife to rub on her chest or apply in her vagina to ease delivery and prevent what the Ijaw call the "stretching" sickness. This malady, described as any serious illness during which the baby stiffens its arms, proves fatal to many infants. A few women avoid medicine, experience little pain, and occasionally deliver their own children without great difficulty. Nevertheless, unless a woman is caught by surprise while farming away from the village, she will always call for a midwife in case complications requiring her aid arise during delivery. She is assisted by female relatives of the expectant mother.

Several elderly women, qualified by age and experience, act as midwives in Ebiama. Even though one of them has a wide reputation for excellence, neither she nor any of the others are full-time specialists. According to their own descriptions, the midwives use practically the same methods of delivering babies. During parturition, the woman lies down with her legs apart or takes a squatting position. One midwife thinks it helps a woman to walk just before delivery so the baby may be born more quickly. Ordinarily, the mother does not cry out while in labor because, according to the women, she happily anticipates the baby. There is no value assigned to stoical behavior, however, and when in pain, women freely scream, often directing their invective toward sexual relations and their husbands.

Treatment of a difficult birth is of two kinds, depending on whether labor does not begin when expected or whether period of labor is unduly extended. The duration of pregnancy, by Ijaw reckoning, lasts about nine lunar months, but at times it is believed to last as long as fifteen to twenty months. Concern is expressed for those women who look and act as though they should deliver and do not. After a "presser" confirms that parturition is past due a woman usually goes to a diviner to learn the cause of the delay. The explanation most frequently advanced is that an *oru* is at fault. In one case a diviner determined that the pregnant woman had made an agreement with Wọnyinghi to die after she gave birth. At the same time, he also saw that an *oru* had agreed to protect the woman from harm and was, therefore, sustaining her pregnancy. Ceremonies had to be performed both to change the agreement and to compensate the *oru* for its protection.

The other kind of difficulty involves physical problems during labor that call for a midwife to be ready to apply one treatment after another. Reputedly, an expert can turn the head of the foetus downward, if this has not occurred of its own accord, by pressing the stomach. When the pelvic bones are thought to be too narrow, "pressers" will try to spread them. On occasion men are called in to hold a woman upside down and twist her in an attempt to correct the position of the foetus. Ordinarily, men are not allowed to be in the room during parturition, since the genitals of a woman should never be seen by a male other than her husband.

Besides using physical manipulation, midwives appeal for aid to the *tẹmẹ* of dead midwives or of anyone else whom they think might help. Women having a difficult labor are also asked to confess any invocations they may have made improperly that could have offended *orumọ*. The *orumọ* are promised drink in return for easing delivery.

Bull-roarers were once spun in the bush near the houses of women having trouble during their labor to frighten them into giving birth quickly. The sound was supposed to represent a strange, fearful, and indescribable creature from the forest that would obviously harm anyone it caught. A man who demonstrated the use of bull-roarers explained that in the past only men were allowed to see them but now, since women and young boys know the source of the sounds as well, they are no longer employed.

POST-PARTUM TREATMENT

After parturition the midwife cuts the umbilical cord at the length of about eight inches, a "hand's length" from the navel, using any blade available. For a male child the midwife makes two strokes with the knife as though to cut, and actually does so on the third; the cord on the female is cut on the fourth stroke. This distinction is the first in a series of acts throughout life which invariably associates the number three with a male and four with a female. Despite the feeling that odd numbers are good while even numbers are bad, Ijaw assert that the association of numbers with sex is mainly to distinguish males from females and not to evaluate the sexes. If there is any delay in expulsion of the afterbirth, the midwife presses the mother's stomach. She immediately buries the placenta in the house, being careful not to leave a hint of its precise location and not to look at it after it has been deposited in the hole for fear of going blind.

During this time, the other women will have ground dried mud into a powder for use as an abrasive to cleanse the baby before washing him with soap and water. It is believed that without proper washing the child will exude an unpleasant odor for the rest of his life. Finally, the infant is rubbed with palm oil or pomade. To stop the umbilical cord from bleeding, its stump is treated with ashes and tied with raffia. The cord drops off in three to seven days, though the process may be hastened by putting leaves and gunpowder on the navel of the infant. The cord is buried outside the house, sometimes near a productive plantain tree, other times simply in a refuse heap.

Men and children cannot see the mother and the new child until after the infant has been washed. The danger of a *diriguǫkęmę* killing the infant by "eyeing" him is recognized but no restrictions on visitors or precautionary hiding occur except in the case of the *orumǫ* priests. They may not see the deciduous hair of a newly born infant, the cord before it drops, nor the exposed breasts of the mother, since if these taboos are violated, either the baby will die or the *oru* priest will fall ill. A typical explanation for this belief is that "this is the way the *oru* wants it." A few individuals imply that a priest's *oru* harms an infant, while the priest experiences danger because he has not followed the wishes of the *oru*.

After washing the mother and baby, the midwife lightly presses the woman's stomach with her foot, three times for a boy and four times for a girl, to prevent any painful after-effects. This ends the midwife's responsibilities. She returns for her payment in three or four days, depending on the sex of the infant, at the same time the whole village is summoned to drink in celebration of the birth. In earlier days the father provided three jars of palm wine at the birth of a boy, or four jars for a girl, and he gave a corresponding three or four shillings to the midwife. By the time of this field study, the provisions and fee had changed to three jars and three shillings for the midwife, irrespective of the sex of the baby. (One jar of palm wine is shared by the men and two jars by the women, since the Ijaw say the latter work more at the birth.) The father of a newly born infant thought the earlier variation in amounts was only to distinguish sex and was changed to reduce costs. If the infant dies before this rite, the midwife receives no payment.

The child's head is shaved at this time because it is "the custom and the way our ancestors did it" as far as most of the villagers are concerned. One man ventured a guess that baby hair is brought from the world of the dead and therefore should be removed. As with the ubiquitous numbers three and four, head-shaving occurs several times during the life cycle, appearing finally at the burial. After the infant has been shaved, *oru* priests can see him and the mother's breasts without danger. Christians follow the same pattern in celebrating the birth of a child, but they say the head-shaving can occur on any day.

In the past, twins and breech presentations were killed by throwing them in the river or by placing them in fish traps and exposing them in the forest. Malformed infants, or those born with teeth were undesirable, but not abandoned. Under threats of punishment from the Government, and with the Christians of the village threatening to report anyone to the police for not observing the regulation, breech-birth babies have been allowed to live, but there is still a strong antipathy toward twins. One twin born to non-Christians has survived in Ebiama, and the Christians hope they themselves will have twins. Despite this changing attitude, a mother of twins must still avoid all *orumǫ* and their officials until she aborts, miscarries, or bears another child. Her husband undergoes the same restrictions for a similar period of time, unless one of his other wives gives birth earlier.

During the seven-day period following a normal birth, the mother and baby are not supposed to leave the house. The place of confinement depends upon where assistance is available, which usually means either the paternal residence of the woman, the house of a friend or, if her co-wives will help her or her mother will come, her own home. A woman from another village also anticipates help from women of her home settlement who have married Ebiama men. As in most situations, post-partum aid is given on a reciprocal basis, and a woman finds herself alone if she has not helped her own sisters or other women at the time of their deliveries.

At the end of the confinement period, if a woman delivers in someone else's house, she and her infant return without ceremony to her own domicile. The length of time she remains in her house without having to go to her farms depends on how well her husband and his relatives, or her own family, take care of her. Should no one be able to bring her food, and if her own stores are small, the period may be as short as ten days. Cases of women having to go to their farms within three weeks are not uncommon, but for the most part a woman will not have to farm for two to three months or until she feels ready to work again. By that time, the infant is strong enough to hold up his head while carried on his mother's back to the fields.

The Ijaw concern for children receives further emphasis in the measures employed to prevent illness. In one case a man and his wife did not appear at the social gathering on the fourth day after the birth of their daughter because their previous daughters had died after a comparable celebration. By not celebrating, that is, by avoiding the customary practice, the parents believed history might not be repeated. This reasoning is reflected in a number of parallel incidents. A father withheld naming his child for several years because previous ones had died after being named. Many men put off the time for circumcising their sons after earlier ones had died, even though their deaths had no obvious relationship to the circumcision. The ceremony of shaving the baby's head can be postponed for weeks if a change seems desirable. Besides postponing rites, a great amount of medical aid is applied, including dropping various herbal mixtures in the eyes of the baby to prevent the "stretching" illness, giving daily dosages of cure-all patent medicines, and spitting gin on the baby to make him strong.

4/Childhood from birth to four: the age of dependence

OR THE FIRST FOUR YEARS of his life, the Ijaw child lives in a world composed of individuals prepared and willing to care for all his needs and to protect him. His presence is a source of pleasure and pride to his parents and kinsmen. Therefore, from birth until the time he can swim, an act demonstrating his ability to cope with an ever present source of danger in the habitat, he is rarely left alone. Since learning to swim and to perform a number of other tasks reduce dependence at about the age of four for most children, our first dividing line will be drawn at that point.

Weaning, almost always coincident with the birth of a younger sibling, provides a subdivision within this span of time. Ideally, this event occurs when the child is at least two years old and able to graduate to a social environment made up of adults and older children who now share with his mother the role of provider and protector. In this older subperiod certain of his demands begin to be met less promptly than before, and prohibitions and punishments begin to transcribe limits to his manipulable world.

During this age-period the child learns basic physical skills and behavior considered minimal for becoming a social member of the household. Estimates of what cultural traits are internalized must be deductive, since most of what we can discover about the learning experiences of young children is through observation of behavior and opinions from parents.

BREAST-FEEDING PERIOD

From birth to weaning the average child in Ebiama begins to demonstrate bodily and emotional control, experiences teething, shifts to a non-milk diet, and learns to walk. Individual variation obviously occurs. This fact must continuously be kept in mind, though differences are minimized by the parents themselves, who believe there are definite and proper ways of training an infant. Unlike the belief that breaking ritual patterns at birth will prove beneficial, any mother, particularly a young one, who deviates from accepted practices is criticized by other women since violating these practices is held to be not only bad in itself but dangerous for the health of the child.

Following a normal birth the mother gives all her attention to the baby. To show his pleasure her husband will purchase new clothes for her and the infant. Even a poor man at least buys his wife a cloth to use in carrying the infant on her back. People from all parts of the village come to visit the mother and admire the child. Opinions as to his physical attractiveness are voiced honestly and the mother accepts these without a show of feeling.

The mother nurses the infant whenever he cries, and as he grows older the breast becomes as much a pacifier as it is a source of nourishment. A woman without milk will try rubbing various kinds of medicine on her breasts, and if these fail, she visits the diviner to receive advice on the cause and remedy. If relief cannot be found, the child usually dies, even though bottle feeding is now sometimes used. Wet nurses are not considered to be an alternative, since it is impossible to persuade a woman to give up her own work to be present at all times. Another woman, however, may occasionally breast-feed a baby when the mother must be absent.

A new mother resumes cooking and weaving mats within two weeks after parturition, but she still devotes a great deal of time to fondling her infant and playing with him. She immediately stops any work she may be doing to give him attention; indeed, she refrains from activities that would interfere with such care. Her husband also plays with the child on returning home from the forest each evening.

An infant is bathed in hot water at least once a day, more often two or three times, and then rubbed with pomade. The mother cups the bath water in her hand and splashes it over the baby's face, forcing him to swallow some of the water. She purposely bathes the baby often because she thinks the child is thirsty, even though infants subjected to the process usually wail loudly.

Infants are not diapered and, for at least the first three months of their lives, never disturbed while they eliminate because Ijaw believe movement might frighten them into stopping. The anus is cleaned with water by the mother or one of the older children and the feces thrown into the river or the forest. Sometimes dogs are called to eat them. One woman allows the dogs to lick clean her infant's anus as well, but other women think this revolting. Ijaw are supposed to use only the left hand in cleaning themselves, but several women were observed catching the feces of their infants in their right hands. Urine is rubbed into the mud floor with the bare foot. Although the bodily functions of a child at this early age are treated casually, and the excreta evoke no avoidance or repulsion, an infant must not be allowed to touch his feces. In earlier times when a baby ate his feces, the mother or father would also have to eat it, since Ijaw believed that unless this were done the child would die. "Eating" the feces consisted of touching the spot on the ground where they had been and then touching the tongue. An elderly women in her seventies saw this done in her youth, but she has never had the occasion to do it herself. Younger women and men know of, but ignore, the practice since they do not believe it can affect a child's welfare.

Throughout the day or night the child is nursed whenever he cries. After a mother resumes farming, the attention she pays her infant does not diminish appreciably. He remains with her while she works, either tied to her back with a cloth or placed on a mat on the ground if she or one of her older children is close by. Although a two- or three-months-old baby is old enough to be carried easily, a woman tries to restrict her economic activities, avoiding long fishing trips or communal fishing expeditions because she frequently would have to stop her work to feed the baby. Nevertheless, some mothers are accused of using their infants as an excuse for not participating in difficult ventures such as trap-fishing during the annual flood.

Many women readily acknowledge that the demands of an infant can be used as an excuse to refrain from sexual intercourse. If a man is unable to persuade his wife to have sexual relations earlier, intercourse usually resumes after the second month, when the baby is perceived to smile. At this and other times a woman wishing to avoid coition will pinch her baby to make him cry, and then proceed to tend him until her husband falls asleep.

Until the child begins to walk at about the age of a year, he is carried everywhere, either by holding him straddled on the hip or tied to the back. To tie a baby on her back the mother slips the child around her hip, leans slightly forward, and balances him while she uses both hands to tie the cloth. Since being carried on the back is believed to cause the infant discomfort, older children are frequently allowed to carry him until his legs are spread and he becomes accustomed to the position. An infant rarely falls, but if he should, his mother must "pay a penalty" by providing a meal for the children living nearby. In return they "tell the mother's back" not to let it happen again, and thereby the infant knows his mother still loves him. The mother's responsibility for the welfare of her child is part of a complex of beliefs which includes the practice of tasting the feces mentioned earlier and the requirement that a woman give a bottle of gin to the members of her subsection if her infant burns or cuts himself. Furthermore, before a child's first tooth erupts, the mother must be careful not to enter certain portions of the forest belonging to *orumọ*, nor allow the baby to see himself in a mirror for fear he will see his agreement with Wọnyinghi and die immediately.

Until the teeth of an infant appear, he is not considered fully human, and if he dies before this time, he will be buried in "bad bush"—a portion of the forest reserved for such deaths—without clothes or coffin. A much less important requirement for achieving the status of a human being is that at some time the infant contract yaws. Three months after a male has yaws, or four months in the case of a girl, the head is shaved, whether or not the child is cured by that time. Now, being a whole person, he has the right to a proper burial.

Teething   In Ebiama the cutting of a first tooth is one of three main events in the life of a boy; circumcision and climbing an oil-palm tree for the first time are the two other occasions acknowledged as requisite for admission to adult status. For a girl no other event besides teething is recognized ritually until she marries. When the first lower tooth is noticed, usually between the fifth and seventh month, no one is supposed to comment until the baby has been taken to an old man of the village who says, "Let the tooth not disappear." Without these precautions it is believed that the tooth may recede, perhaps called away by other children, and never appear again. Before the advent of British rule a child whose upper teeth appeared first was killed or sold as a slave to the Nembe. During the time this practice has been prohibited by the Government individuals whose upper teeth appeared first have grown up in the village and married without difficulty.

After teething, the child's head is shaved completely, and three or four days later, depending on sex, the new hair is trimmed, with half of the scalp divided into three sections for a male or four sections for a female. If not enough hair has grown to trim, the mother places mud on the head of the child and shaves that off instead. She then decorates his scalp with chalk marks and a headtie, places beads around his waist, and walks about the village with him. Villagers give the infant pennies and food which are happily accepted by his parent. The baby is in no danger if the ceremony is not performed, but other women will criticize the mother for what appears to them to be neglect of her child.

Naming   Most parents name their children at about the same time the ceremony is performed for the first tooth. The father summons friends and relatives of both sexes to his house, serves drinks, and in the presence of his wife and child announces the name. The gathering greets this with approval and offers presents ("dashes") of a penny to a shilling. The father might ask that the name of each donor be recorded in a notebook, though he himself cannot read. Drinking then continues into the night. The recording of gifts represents an innovation which is also observed at funerals. It is done "for the record," rather than because of an explicit desire to keep an accurate account of reciprocal presents in the future.

Everything about the naming is arbitrary including the name itself. There need be no celebration at all, or if the naming of one child is celebrated, this does not have to be done for the next. It depends on a man's wealth, his attitude toward the ceremony, his health, the time of the year, and the amount of palm wine available.

Ijaw names are descriptive and often refer to circumstances surrounding the birth of the child. Alatimi (remained-a-long-time) received his name because his mother was pregnant with him longer than nine months. The parents of a girl called Oweizighẹ (a-boy-has-not-been-born) were hoping for a boy. Several children bear names that are variations of "God's Gift" because their births were eagerly anticipated. A child can be named after an ancestor to honor him or to ask him for protection. A number of instances are encountered in which a child is given the name of a deceased older sibling. Although dead children are believed sometimes to be reincarnated in subsequent siblings, parents practicing duplicate naming agree they do so to keep the number of names in the family at a minimum, not because they believe in reincarnation. Mother, father, or, indeed, anyone may suggest a name. An infant can also receive a nickname based on a physical or behavioral idiosyncrasy, but he soon becomes known by only one of his names. English names are in fashion in the village and are chosen by non-Christians, as well as Christians, as any other name might be.

Another innovation, reinterpreted from English usage, is the adoption by an individual of his father's name. A child named Alatimi, for example, whose father is Tebi, will be called Alatimi Tebi; Alatimi's child, named Owei, would be called Owei Alatimi, or, very infrequently and only when the grandfather is a man of some prestige, Owei Tebi.

Walking and Toilet Training   Despite the change in status following teething, the treatment accorded an infant by the household continues as before. His cries bring immediate attention, and his movements are rarely physically restricted. By the age of seven months he should be able to sit erect, but a mother can facilitate this by supporting him with pillows in a basin. The infant is allowed to touch everything, including any part of his own body. Only when a child crawls near the kitchen fire is he restrained. His mother gently moves him to one side or asks an older child or co-wife to distract him while she continues her cooking. To permit the baby to learn by burning himself is considered too dangerous, and the mother would be punished by having to pay a bottle of gin to her husband's kinsmen. Restraint occurs in other unusual and infrequent circumstances. For example, a child is discouraged from trying to walk before he has teethed because this sequence is believed to be the wrong order of development. A baby is also not supposed to eat mashed food before teething, but a mother often acquiesces to his demand even though other women jokingly call him greedy for asking to eat while so young.

As a child approaches the age of walking, between a year and eighteen months old, toilet-training subtly begins and preparations are made for weaning. At night the mother senses the needs of the infant by his movements and places him on the floor to urinate. Some mothers report having "trained" their children in this way by the age of eleven or twelve months, but from the difficulties observed with older children, it seems reasonable to assume that these mothers are better trained in anticipation than their offspring in restraint. No preference is expressed whether toilet-training should be completed before or after weaning. Since weaning occurs abruptly, toilet-training often continues after nursing has stopped. Once the child can walk and communicate with his mother, she tells him to go to the side of the house to defecate. She will still dispose of the feces and clean the child, and at night she tells him to call her when he wishes to urinate. Before the age of three he is not punished physically if he fails to respond, but subsequent mistakes are treated with increasing severity.

Encouragement to walk is casually given, perhaps because sitting up and walking are neither anticipated with enthusiasm nor celebrated, but simply accepted as normal human development. A baby is held by the hands and occasionally a stroller is built for him. After learning to walk, he transcends, practically for the first time, the unitary sphere of intimate relationship with his mother. A variety of persons may now care for him while she goes for brief periods to farm or is occupied in the house. An older sibling is most often selected to look after him, but if one is not available, then a co-wife, husband, or mother will be called. They continue to be permissive, providing food or attention whenever he cries.

Once the child is walking, everyone must be particularly watchful that he does not go to the river, since the banks are fairly steep and children have tumbled down them and have drowned. Mishaps of this sort are rare but their possibility provokes repeated warnings to the parental surrogate to exercise caution with his ward when near the water.

Crying At about the same time children learn to walk with ease, they are subjected to physical punishment and threats if they cry unreasonably. Adults believe a young child will become ill from continual weeping, but the noise obviously aggravates the mother and spurs her to action. The example of a year-and-a-half-old boy illustrates various techniques to stop a child from crying, though typically fewer are used at any one time.

> Ikiye and his parents are watching a curing ceremony. He begins to wail because he is irritated or wants attention. At first his mother offers her breast, which he refuses, as he does the food next given him. His crying becomes more intense as

his mother strikes him with a small stick. A women takes him to the waterside and holds him under for short periods. This is still without avail, so she places him under a fishing basket. He becomes terrified. Another woman comes and acting the part of one saving him from his captor, rushes him to his mother. He now takes her breast and is quiet.

Most women state they would not go so far as to pretend to drown a child, nor would they suspend him by his ankles, a technique reported but never observed, to halt his weeping since these measures are held to be dangerous. Threats are the most common disciplinary means used.

Two different kinds of threats are to be distinguished: those promising an undefinable punishment and those in which the promise of punishment is potentially real. In the first category parents usually are simply trying to stop a child from crying or to divert his attention from something he wants by frightening him. The threat frequently used by adults is that "something is coming." The intonation of the voice, more than the indescribable "something" (*iyei*), frightens most infants and stops their crying. An actual object such as a goat or a dog will also be named if the parents have noticed that their child was once frightened by one of these. "An *owu* (masked dancer) will get you" might be another threat, though this one is not often employed. The threats are effective for a child who has not yet learned to speak because parents are easily able to dramatize these agents.

Threats in the second category are usually more persuasive after a child has been weaned. An uncircumcised boy may be warned that he will have an operation immediately if he does not stop his crying. A mother may threaten to rub pepper or mentholatum in his eyes, or to tell his father about his bad behavior. Finally, a passerby can be asked to pretend to take a knife and cut off the child's head.

Practically the only beings which almost all mothers feel should not be used as threats are the dead and the *orumọ*. Two young mothers who had no experience in handling older children expressed the opinion that given enough provocation they might call on the dead, but a third disagreed because she could remember during her own childhood how frightened she had been of them. All other women queried, who had older children, agreed that it was bad to refer to the dead and *orumọ* as disciplining agents. One of them explained that these beings might consider themselves invoked and implement the threat.

These modes of discipline refer to cases of children crying continuously and without justifiable reason. A child crying because he has been physically hurt is gently treated. The mother "begs" him to stop, using the typical expression for adult mishaps, "sorry" (*dilẹ*), and promises him some delicacy he enjoys.

WEANING

Techniques for weaning are similar to those used to quiet a youngster who cries without reason. Parents say they stop their children from crying for the breast by frightening them with the name of a fearsome person, by threatening that an airplane or a white man will take them away, or by promising to summon an *owu*. These threats are ordinarily used in conjunction with applying a distasteful substance to the nipples, such as a wild plant called "bitter leaves," potash, white chalk, or some bitter-tasting patent medicine. To the disgust of many mothers who heard what she had done, one woman reports having placed a millipede on her breast to frighten her child.

Weaning begins at the onset or during the first few months of an ensuing pregnancy. This means that most infants are breast-fed for at least two years, and to stop much before this time is considered unhealthy for the child. There are cases of mothers, who did not expect to become pregnant again, nursing a last child for as long as four years, but this also is thought to be unwholesome and is referred to as "an old custom." Usually weaning occurs abruptly, often within five days. Food or palm wine is always offered as a pacifier whenever the child cries during this period. A persistent child may be sent away for a few days, ordinarily to his maternal grandmother.

A change in the relations between mother and child appears to take place swiftly, but actually the final break, induced by the use of bitter substances, comes after a slow transition. As the mother goes to farm, she begins to leave her offspring at home for short periods so that he becomes less dependent on her. Solid foods have become the major part of the child's diet. These include foods easily handled by the child: tidbits of mashed cocoyams, plantain, and boned fish. After weaning, he is always left at home unless his mother cannot find someone to watch over him. With walking he made his first physical move out of a single sphere of relationship with his mother. Weaning completes the severance of total dependence, particularly if a new sibling now attracts his mother's attention and forces him to rely on other individuals.

Even though the suckling period has no Ijaw name nor can "weaning" be expressed in other than descriptive terms, *ndo pęlę* (to stop from the breast), for convenience of analysis it provides a good point at which to pause and review what the infant has learned thus far. Most of his learned behavior pertains to bodily and emotional control: walking, toilet-training, eating, and crying. Although the processes of acquiring these habits have significance for the shaping of personality, they cannot be empirically related to cultural modes of thought and behavior. While there may be some question as to why a pre-five-year-old stops crying at the mention of an *owu*, because of the intonation of his mother's voice or because the term is associated with what frightens him, there is no evidence to lead us to suspect that he is afraid of *owumọ* because they may represent deities from the river. Ijaw themselves conceive of this early training not as being directly related to the knowledge of *owumọ*, but simply as a means to accomplish overt objectives: weaning and self-control of tears.

Little else is expected of the child during this initial period. Whatever cultural and social traits he learns appear to the observer as bits and pieces of adult behavior, the acquisition of which depends on the precocity of individual children. For example, one man not only tried to have his son, aged one and a half years, return a match box that he threw some distance in play, but he also told him to bow or "bend the knee" and return it with his right hand. A parent instructs his child in these "good manners" by having him imitate an older child. Whenever he performs successfully, he is greeted with smiles and commendation. Similarly, a few children begin to take what looks like dance steps and to act as though they know how to share food. Both are received with enthusiastic approval. During a dance, the first steps a youngster takes are immediately noticed and all those present clap with the rhythm and call out encouragement. A child learns to share in much the same way. At first the mother shares her own food with her child and later, whenever he has food that can be divided, like sugar cane, she asks him to give her some, and praises him warmly for it. If he refuses, he is gently reprimanded and the food is taken from him and given to others.

NEW SURROGATES

The second phase of this initial period extends from the time the child is weaned, at about the age of two, to the time he learns to swim, perform household tasks, and become somewhat independent. It is mainly characterized by a shift in supervision from the mother to older children and by the child learning to talk. Adults believe that the child now begins the final part of the transition from an infant world, in which he has close contact with the souls of the unborn and the dead, to the reality of the adult world where direct association with the unseen is usually limited to diviners.

The birth of a younger sibling is an important event for the two- to four-year-old child. According to mothers' reports and our own observations, children react in different ways to a new baby:

> Oyibo, aged three, appears to dislike her new sister. She cries to get attention and demonstrates her pleasure when anyone takes the infant from her mother. Two boys, aged three and two and a half, always play with their infant siblings, but the younger one sometimes cries and creates difficulties while eating to attract notice from his mother.

Mothers say they anticipate potential antagonisms and try not to ignore an older sibling. At this time, however, they impose harsh physical punishment for bad behavior and thereby emphasize their shift of interest to the younger child.

With his mother paying less attention to him because of his new sibling, the child enters relationships controlled by other people. His mother still continues to be the most important personage for his well being, responsible for his food and comfort and for instructions concerning his care, but the task of watching him, playing with him, and attending to his immediate needs is most frequently given to an older brother or sister. A child as young as eight is believed capable of assuming some responsibility for him, but one older, who has more physical strength and experience, would be called upon to bathe him and cook for him.

If a woman has no older children, she can ask a kinsman, preferably her sister's daughter, to live with her and care for her child in return for food and clothing. A mother may also ask a co-wife or some other unrelated woman in the village for the services of her daughter. Whenever possible the pre-five-year-old child lives in the same house as his parents, sleeping in the same room with his mother but in another bed or on a mat laid on the floor, once a new baby comes. Shifting from one household or village to another, however, is not atypical in this period of life. Some of these changes are only temporary, as when an infant being weaned is sent to live with his maternal grandmother. Less frequently, the change is for the full time of his childhood. If no one is available to help care for the child, he might be sent to another house or village to live with kinsmen, particularly a woman with older children of her own.

Although residence is virilocal and ideally patrilocal, agnates are not the only kinsmen to take part in training a child. With the high frequency of intravillage marriages, relatives of both parents are involved. Men feel free to punish their own offspring as well as a child related to them through their brother or sister. Women, however, express a different opinion, saying they would beat their sisters' children but hesitate to strike those of their brothers. The difference rests on the degree of significance attributed to the relationship between the mother's brother and his sister's son. Men believe that in the past a father could not strike harshly even his own son by a small-dowry marriage without fear of being reprimanded by his wife's brother. They no longer feel any restraint even though the inheritance rules retain a matrilineal emphasis.

Parents say they would be pleased if someone struck their progeny for doing something bad. In practice this is not the case and a quarrel could easily ensue. A woman who beats her co-wife's child or her husband's brother's child reports her action to his parents as quickly as possible to allay any misunderstanding.

By describing physical punishments and disciplining agents, "bad behavior" on the part of the child may seem more emphasized for this age-period than is warranted. The Ijaw conceptions of "good" or "bad" crystallize only for older children whose behavior depends more explicitly on rewards and punishments. The misbehavior of a two to four-year-old boy or girl is similar to that which provokes parents to threaten to use physical force on a younger, unweaned child. One who cries for something he wants and cannot have is punished by the same means. Young children have little opportunity to act in ways considered "bad," such as breaking plates or secretly taking food, because they are constantly in the company of older surrogates.

The few demands for proper behavior that are backed with corporal punishment are rarely enforced. The surrogate, particularly a young sibling, usually refers a child's misbehavior back to his parents. Since these young guardians are as responsible for their charges as an older person would be, parents are inclined to blame them for anything that goes wrong. Therefore, a girl does not wish to make her ward cry without good reason for she in turn may be punished by her mother.

The responses of children to adults other than their parents or guardians vary considerably. Some youngsters are suspicious and fearful of strangers and refuse to accept gifts of food from them, while others are friendly and readily accept anything offered. Parents encourage reticence because they are afraid their children may be given poisoned food. For the most part a child of this age seldom must make the distinction between those from whom he should or should not accept food.

SKILLS

By the age of four, a child has learned how to eat expertly with his hands, a skill that applies mainly to eating "foofoo" or "gari." (Foofoo is a thick paste made from cooked cassava. Gari is dried cassava meal made into a paste by adding boiling water.) Both are rolled into small balls with the right hand alone and used to soak up soup. At the same time he becomes artful in eating, he is encouraged to share his food with others. When several children eat together, arguments sometimes arise over who is taking more by eating too quickly. Parents rebuke signs of selfishness, and even when eating alone a child should show self-restraint. On one occasion a woman threatened to beat her son unless he finished his food because he had been greedy and asked for more than he could eat.

Little distinction is made between the sexes in the training and treatment of pre-five-year-olds with the exception of physical modesty. Both boys and girls are almost always nude, but a girl is taught not to sit with her legs apart and not to bend at the waist without wearing a cloth. These precepts are persistent and everyone immediately corrects a girl for carelessly exposing her genitals.

A child learns to paddle by playing with miniature paddles either purchased or crudely carved. He takes the paddle with him whenever he travels by canoe. At other times, he pretends to be in a canoe and practices paddling while he straddles a bench or the railing of a verandah. Adults correct him if he is holding the paddle wrongly or performing awkwardly. Although a child of four is too weak to help in paddling a canoe, many of this age are able to hold the rhythm, even when the tempo is rapid, and imitate the motions of adults. Parents and older children always encourage the child by saying "thank you" (*noao*) or by complimenting his performance.

To help boys and girls learn the use of a machete, they are urged to weed grass growing near the house. Sharp, miniature knives are used, but a mother is relieved of paying fines for injuries incurred by any of her children older than the age of three since they are now more removed from her constant care. Yet, a tale women like to repeat indicates a continual feeling of personal responsibility for any harm befalling their offspring. Briefly, the story tells of a mother who failed to teach her son to be careful with knives so that one day, while he was playing, he cut off his penis. The son did not realize the consequences of his accident until he tried to marry and found no woman would accept him. He therefore killed his mother because her neglect brought about his misfortune, and then he committed suicide.

PLAY-GROUPS

Near the age of weaning, the child begins to watch other boys and girls play games. Since their activities distract him from continuously calling for his mother, adults encourage older children to respond to his presence and bring him into their games as much as possible. Toward the end of this age-period, the children begin to congregate in their own play-groups. They must always remain within calling distance of their guardians, but they gradually become more independent for longer periods of time. Their games principally consist of sporadic and simple imitation, almost like follow-the-leader. In one play-group a girl, age four, was obviously the leader of several others, even though two of them were several months older than she.

Ere instructs the other children to follow her to sleep, and they all lie down and pretend to sleep; then she tells them to play "mosquito net," so they pull a cloth over themselves. After a short time they tire of this, get up, and Ere suggests they urinate, which they all proceed to do.

Aside from the paddles mentioned above, games are notable for their absence of toys which are rarely seen in the village. Only one four-year-old girl plays with a doll, an Igbo wood carving that her mother bought in Port Harcourt. Other girls occasionally pretend that uncarved pieces of wood are babies and tie them to their backs with cloths.

The composition of the play-groups is dependent on the amicability of its members as much as on residence and age. With quarreling a commonplace occurrence in the daily life of adults, the four-year-old children begin to follow suit. The source of an argument between them is usually obscure, but a series of insults intensifies whatever difference or misunderstanding may have been initially present. The technique of exchanging insults is not hard to learn, particularly since they are echoed everywhere. They include everything from a simple blinking of the eye or crying, "your big head," to the more sophisticated expressions adults use to reveal something personally shameful, and perhaps unknown to the community: "Ege urinates in bed," or, "Imi has few pubic hairs." Children try to insult each other by referring to obvious personal characteristics, such as unsightly yaws. At this stage the insults are often said incorrectly to the delight of older children, and arguments usually end in a wrestling bout because an insufficient number of insults is known to keep them going for any length of time.

These wrestling matches are miniature replicas of an adult fracas. After a brief scuffle that attracts others who separate them, the combatants continue their insults, demand a return to the struggle, and if they remember the original reason for the fight, loudly explain to those present their side of the argument. If the children are of the same age and size—sex is not a factor—they are allowed to continue a match until one is thrown. The onlookers then quickly separate the two and lead each home, though the loser usually struggles and cries to return and continue.

Arguments and fights at this age are treated very lightly by parents unless a child is continuously contentious. In that case restraint is suggested and, if ignored, he is punished. Parents are seriously concerned only when a son or daughter runs away from an encounter. A youth may cry and plead not to return to the match, but his parents will either force him to wrestle or give him a beating. The reaction of adults can be seen in part as projection of their impatience with the child's cries, a situation resulting in physical punishment even of a toddler; but principally it pertains to a larger issue of being a true Ijaw.

One who runs away from a fight is *su*, which English-speaking Ijaw translate as "lazy," but which more accurately describes someone who will not, or is physically unable to, perform certain basic tasks expected of everyone in the community. In other words, an individual is not being Ijaw; he is "inadequate" or "inefficient." *Su*, defined in these terms, has a different connotation from what might ordinarily be interpreted as cowardice, since fear of pain or danger is not the issue. A child or an adult is permitted to cry at the slightest pain, caused by illness or by application of a medicine to a wound. Demonstrating fear of a snake by running from one in the forest is condoned. But to run from a fight is different, and observations confirm that parents punish their children for this misbehavior in practice as much as they claim to in the abstract. The only exceptions occur when other adults advise a parent to temper his demands, since the child may not yet understand what is expected of him.

"POWER" OF CHILDREN

Before leaving this stage, mention should be made again of the belief in the power (*kro*) of the children, since on reaching an age of knowing right from wrong, this power leaves them. *Kro* denotes the ability of a child to understand the speech of infants, to see ghosts and the *tẹmẹ* of unborn children, to remember how he lived before his birth or reincarnation, and to help women conceive. In the view of some Ijaw a pre-five-year-old is on the border between the worlds of the dead (*duwoiama*) and the living, and *krọ* represents his ability to function in both. Prior to the time he can speak, his power is deduced from his actions. For example, a baby who cries for no apparent reason is held to be seeing ghosts, and is, therefore, moved to another room; or he might cry out on seeing the spirits of unborn children coming to his mother, because he is jealous and wants no siblings.

After an infant learns to talk, he may indicate possession of *kro* by reciting long tales of travels before his birth, or the circumstances of his several deaths before he finally decided to remain in the world of the living. Children often scatter food on the ground and parents interpret this as their offspring sharing it with invisible friends. One mother, who reported this behavior for her four-year-old daughter, added that when the girl dreamed, she would talk in her sleep and ask for the return of this food. A child can also indicate the personal taboos on which his life depends, such as not being taken to localities where the dead are laid out before burial.

According to Ijaw belief, as we have seen, the soul (*tẹmẹ*) of an individual exists before his birth and after his death. The line between the worlds of the living and the non-living is not drawn at birth nor even with the entrance of a *tẹmẹ* into the womb of a woman. Having a body, a complete one in the sense of also having teeth, is the necessary first step toward becoming a part of the living world; acquiring "culture" and morality is the sufficient and final step. The termination of *krọ*, for all people except possibly diviners, signifies the beginning of conscious memory and, in the estimation of adults, the time children should know right from wrong, particularly with regard to stealing and lying. If the child survives through this age-period his parents seem to acknowledge his choice of joining the living, rather than returning to those who are not alive, by being less anxious about his health. They grant him more independence in his movements and more severe punishments for not participating as an Ijaw should in the world of the living.

An aspect of this belief in the special powers of children becomes evident at the time of sickness. If a child has a long serious illness, a variety of herbal and patent medicines are given him and a diviner is summoned to give a diagnosis.

The diviner has a broad repertoire of causes to draw upon, but two of the most common are that the child made an agreement with Wǫnyinghi to die at a young age, his present illness presaging his impending death; and second, that an *oru* is at fault because it wants the child to serve it. In the first case, the diviner performs a ceremony for the patient to change the agreement. In the second, offerings are made to the *oru* and its priest employs divination to establish the reason for its choice of this particular child. Generally, the *oru* reveals either that the parents have failed to keep a promise to propitiate it for some past favor, or that the deity has simply expressed its wish to have this child as one of its followers. In the latter case, his father or mother must occasionally bring gin or palm wine to the *oru* until the child is old enough to enter the cult-house himself. In return the *oru* is expected to allow the patient to recover and to protect him in the future. Adults claim that children gaining protection in this way would not be treated in an exceptional way, though possibly their parents might hesitate to beat them for fear of offending the *oru*. During the course of our investigation no children were placed in this special relationship with an *oru*.

Another diagnosis, particularly relevant for a child of this age, is that his mother's unborn child is trying to kill him because he wants no siblings or wishes to be the eldest. In some cases the living child "knows" of this hostility on the part of his unborn sibling and attempts to retaliate by causing his mother to miscarry or the infant to die at birth. The living child, on the other hand, may initiate the antagonism or even cause his mother to be barren. In either case the two siblings are thought to compete in their attempts to harm one another, and the stronger of the two will bring about the death of the other unless he is stopped. To accomplish a truce, a covenant ($\varrho vu\varrho$) is made. Any man can initiate a covenant by making a pronouncement to the effect that if either of the two parties to a dispute should "think evilly" of the other or try to harm him, the $\varrho vu\varrho$ itself will kill him. The covenant can also be made more formally in a cult-house where the *oru* is called upon to witness and reinforce the $\varrho vu\varrho$. To represent the agreement, special sticks and nuts are hung around the necks of the child and of the mother, who wears it for the unborn sibling. The woman transfers her neckpiece to the latter after his birth, and both children continue to wear them until the strings break or are lost.

LANGUAGE

Although the child displays few discernible learning achievements of cultural materials during this period, the stage is obviously set for the amorphous child to begin the transformation to being a complete Ijaw. Learning to speak and acquiring a vocabulary are, of course, crucial requirements. Parents accept language development as entirely natural and believe an offspring of Ijaw parents would grow up to speak Ijaw under any circumstances. Knowledge of a language enables a child to learn his culture very rapidly, both by listening to conversation and by asking questions. Ijaw children, however, do not constantly badger their parents with questions. Whenever they manifest a tendency to query the how and why of things, they receive meager encouragement, since adults usually answer with impatience or simply ignore them. Another factor also plays some part in this seeming paucity of curiosity among children. Parents rarely direct the attention of a child to objects about him or explain their use. Inferentially, the Ijaw theory of education is that, insofar as language and cultural traits are concerned, the child learns by observing, listening, and eventually experimenting. Children have every opportunity to do these things, for they are excluded from little that transpires around them. As a result, their cultural world gradually unfolds without their having to ask about it.

After a three- or four-year-old has some facility with language, parents begin to introduce him to preferred patterns of behavior for obedience, sharing, and modesty. Repeated instructions concerning taking food in the house without permission or venturing alone to the river should now be understood, and parents punish a child for disobeying them. Kinship terms are used to address only parents and grandparents. There is no "baby talk," but, unlike many other African societies, the Ijaw have a special child's term for "mother." Children often use the term *nẹnẹ* to refer to mother instead of *nyinghi*. Few other terms are learned at this time probably because adults call most relatives by their personal names, instead of by kinship terms which are reserved primarily for indirect address.

The dependence of the child up to about the age of five is based on the inability of the youngster to care for himself. Coincident with physical immaturity is the adult view that an infant is partially cognizant of the world of the non-living, and therefore needs extra protection. In the next age-period, "the age of transition," the child rapidly builds upon the sparse cultural knowledge he has acquired in his first few years, moving from one end of the continuum marked by complete dependence toward the opposite extreme of independence and responsibility for others younger than himself.

5/Childhood from five to eight: the age of transition

BETWEEN FIVE AND EIGHT YEARS OF AGE, children become independent of constant supervision. This is a transitional period wherein they move from a state of dependence to one in which they rely for the most part upon themselves. The knowledge acquired during their earlier years and their physical development allow children to assume certain responsibilities for their own care, and to begin to learn skills that are of practical use in the household. Despite the diffuse learning experiences of this period, a solid foundation begins to gel for the next big step to becoming an enculturated and socialized Ijaw.

Up to this point the child has primarily learned bodily controls. Now he begins to learn those particular values and prescribed modes of behavior which characterize Ijaw culture. For the first time, the five-year-old must truly begin to distinguish between right and wrong, since he no longer has someone older than himself to bear the responsibility for his misbehavior. This is only one of the ways in which he becomes more aware of his milieu. His experiences extend beyond the house and section to the entire village. He has wider contacts with kinsmen who do not belong to his household. He participates in various rituals. As a member of a play-group, he reenacts many forms of conduct he witnesses in the village.

Although the information children of this age acquire of the total culture is still limited, their growing language facility not only gives them the ability to acquire knowledge, but also allows them to express themselves concerning what they have learned. They can now answer questions as to what they know, sometimes how they have learned it, and even describe what they would do in certain hypothetical situations.

Parents say that the sequence of acquiring skills and values is unimportant. Whether a girl first learns to weave or to cook is irrelevant as long as she can eventually do both. Nevertheless, very little variation is tolerated in the way tasks are performed. The motor behavior associated with paddling a canoe, for example, is precisely defined, and any deviation from it brings derisive comments from onlookers. Those phases of Ijaw life where individual variation is permitted and those where social conformity remains inflexible will be apparent in the discussion that follows.

Two important activities associated with this age-period have changed in recent times. In earlier days, boys were circumcised at about the age of seven or eight; therefore, the event will be described here in its customary place in the life-sequence, even though the operation has come to be performed on infants. The other change is that most children in Ebiama are in school by the age of six. A description of schooling, however, has been left until the whole process of child rearing has been discussed, since the schooling experience affects children of all ages.

PERSONAL CARE

Swimming is an essential skill that lowers the last restrictive barrier for a child, allowing him to rove freely about by himself. Being able to cope with the river is imperative. By doing so, he is allowed to bathe and wash his clothes at the waterside, use the river as a latrine, and eventually fish there. Only one adult in Ebiama cannot swim, reportedly because he was afraid of the water as a child. He is always open to ridicule, not so much because he is considered to be a coward, but because he is an inadequate (*su*) Ijaw in the same way as a person who avoids a fight with his peers. Most children are well on their way to learning to swim by the time they are five years old. A novice receives no particular recognition or reward for proficiency, aside from occasional praise for good performance. Swimming is a new and enjoyable game for the beginner. His parents may try to keep him from swimming too much because they believe staying in the water for lengthy periods brings on illness, but he takes every opportunity during the hot dry season to practice his strokes with his friends.

Prior to learning how to swim, someone must accompany him to the waterside to steady the canoe as he defecates over the side, and to remain on guard should he fall. A five-year-old child becomes responsible for doing these things alone, including washing his anus with the proper hand, his left one. By these accomplishments, adults consider him to be fully toilet-trained. As toilet-training is completed, enuresis may become a problem. From the numerous reports by mothers, we estimate that at one time or another approximately 30 percent of the children "wet the bed." Parents believe their offspring intentionally urinate in their sleep to spoil the bed mat and to punish their mother by making her weave a new one. Boys and girls, on the other hand, claim a frog, or the bed mat itself, speaks to them in their dreams and deceives them into thinking they are outside the house. Adults think the tale amusing, but use both physical punishment and ridicule to enforce their views. A parent may beat the child or rub a hot, stinging substance, such as mentholated ointment or peppers, on his genitals. As a preventive measure some mothers wake the boy or girl every night and send him outside to urinate. A more persistent offender is dressed in odd clothes and forced to walk through the village to receive the ridicule of adults and other children. If all these measures fail, parents suspect he is ill and take him to a diviner for diagnosis and treatment.

At this age a child is expected to bathe with soap at least once a day at the waterside, but few children have to be reminded to do this since they treat bathing as part of swimming. Keeping their clothes clean is another matter, at least as far as the boys are concerned. Women usually have to order their sons to wash their school uniforms which, in fact, are often the only clothing they own. By contrast, girls often try to wash their dresses even before they can swim, in playful imitation of their mothers. Mothers believe that a girl who learns to wash her own clothes also learns to be careful with them. If she should lose them in the water while washing them, she is beaten and perhaps refused a replacement for a time.

SKILLS AND HOUSEHOLD TASKS

Because of their physical development and increased dexterity, children at home and in their play-groups can imitate fairly accurately many adult activities. Their actions often take the form of games. Adults encourage the children to do as well as possible, and both boys and girls of this age are given certain simple household tasks. In earlier periods parents considered a child to be helpful for primarily negative reasons, that is, he helped by not causing trouble. Now, a child can carry a small bottle of water to the house, mornings and evenings, when he returns from his bath. He washes his own plate, at least, and perhaps the dishes of his parents unless this job is reserved for older siblings. He sweeps the house with a short broom made of dried leaves, bending from the waist and moving the broom with the wrist alone—the same motor behavior used by Ijaw to cut grass or weed a farm with a machete. He may also be told to hold a younger sibling while his mother bathes, or to deliver messages or run errands for his father or other adults in the subsection. Children of this age are the messengers most frequently employed since they are readily available.

Boys are free to attempt female activities and it is not considered strange if a boy enjoys them because adults assume he will change his interests as he grows older. We observed, however, that only girls make an obvious effort to learn to weave. At the age of five or six years girls begin to attempt weaving mats and fishing traps. They learn by watching grown women weave. After some time, perhaps even a year, a girl is encouraged to finish weaving a mat her mother or an older sister has started. The next stage is for her to begin on a small mat that will be used for carrying away floor sweepings. Finally, she tries her hand at making the larger bed mats. For the most part, each girl weaves her own mat, but several youngsters may sit together on a verandah while they work. Adults approve of group projects because the girls work longer and learn more quickly helping each other than by weaving alone. After they become fairly proficient, they weave fishing baskets for their mothers, having learned this by weaving smaller ones for themselves.

The girls use their toy baskets at the waterside to catch small minnowlike fish which they boil in sardine tins over small fires outside their homes. Often they have no fish but still boil water and call it "cooking." This play seems to interest only those who are about five years old, and then only for a comparatively short time. Their older playmates, who are already responsible for preparing food, show little interest in the game, and soon they themselves are allowed to practice cooking in the house.

Mothers teach their offspring to cook by having them watch the preparation, add salt to the food, and then taste it for flavor. Small tasks associated with cooking such as peeling cassava are also assigned to them. Though these practices are initially treated as a game, many children learn to prepare simple foods by the time they are eight years old.

Older girls plant sugar cane and plantain behind the village on land adults have cleared to prevent the forest from encroaching on their homes and to discourage wild animals from coming too close. Younger ones, about six or seven years old, occasionally assist in the weeding of these play-farms. This practice in farming techniques encourages children to imitate their mothers in clearing and cutting grass on a real farm, but they usually tire quickly. Consequently, mothers going to farm rarely take children of this age unless they are mature enough to keep a younger sibling entertained.

Both boys and girls join together in mimicking family life in a game called "playhouse," by assuming the roles of father, mother, and children. "Father" plays his part by becoming a palm-cutter and climbing the posts of a house to cut down imaginary bunches of palm fruit, while "mother" fishes in the river and boils water for cooking. On another occasion, they may decide to build a house out of discarded bamboo strips. Small houses are also made of mud, like actual Ijaw structures, but the children, instead of treading the mud with their feet as adults do, pound it to the proper consistency with sticks. Parents believe this method is good practice for children learning to beat foofoo, a cooking procedure they must perform when somewhat older.

Girls practicing the occupations of women earlier than boys the work of men provides an important test of the early learning hypothesis that will be discussed later. The reason for the difference appears to rest in the nature of the work. Boys do not yet· possess the strength needed to extract palm oil, distill gin, trade, or carve canoes, the principal occupations of men. Along with women and girls, boys help in these tasks by picking palm nuts from bunches or carrying cracked palm kernels, and in this way learn some phases of the work. In fishing, men require strength and dexterity to throw nets; boys, therefore, use the same methods as girls. Similarly, in hunting, the boys employ techniques appropriate to the small animals they attempt to kill. Youths build bird traps from bamboo and use slingshots to stun birds, whereas men shoot larger varieties of birds and hunt for antelope, monkey, and other game of this kind in the forest. Hence, boys come to know something about the work of their fathers, but they cannot, in the nature of the case, gain the practical experience that their sisters obtain in tasks they will later be expected to perform as adults.

KINSHIP

By the time he is eight years old, a child know the terms for father and father's brother (*dau*), for mother and mother's sister (*nyinghi or nẹnẹ*), and for grandparents (*opu dau* and *opu nyinghi*). If he is living with his grandmother, he may address her as *nyinghi* or *nẹnẹ* and call his biological mother by her proper name, even though he knows that the woman he calls *nẹnẹ* is his mother's or father's mother. If his mother is dead and another wife of his father cares for him, he calls her *nęnę*, but he is never permitted to regard her as his true mother. While his mother is alive the relations a preadolescent has with her co-wives depend largely on the degree of friendship among these women. A father's wife who is on good terms with his mother and acts kindly toward him might also be called *nęnę*; otherwise only her personal name will be used. What an eight-year-old knows of other kinship terms depends on his place of residence. He will know how to address his mother's brother (*yabę*) if he is living nearby. Children able to recognize the term *yabę* believe it is only a form of address for their mother's male kin, who should be respected like all other adult relatives. They do not yet fully appreciate, for example, that they will eventually inherit property from them or be dependent on them in other ways.

Since all other kinsmen are addressed by their personal names, mature Ijaw indicate whether a brother or sister is a full or half-sibling by using descriptive terms: *kęnę nyinmǫ* (one mother) or *kęnę daubǫ* (one father), respectively. Few children five to eight years old have learned these terminological distinctions. In a polygynous household half-siblings know they do not share the same mother, since usually only their own mother punishes and feeds them. Yet, in contrast to adolescents and adults, children this age fail to discriminate in their behavior between *kęnę nyinmo* and *kęnę daubǫ*.

PLAY-GROUPS

Aside from the few responsibilities for personal care, a child in this age-period spends most of his time playing with his cohorts. It will be recalled that play-groups generally include children of both sexes. Since there are rarely many children of the same age residing close to one another, the play-groups may one day be small, composed of only a few similar in age, and another day comprise children whose ages range from five to eight, or even older. An older child may act as instructor or leader but he will not order the others about or beat them. If he were to do so, children explain, younger ones would refuse to play with him.

Learning about Sex   Adults realize that children in this age-period are beginning to learn about sex, but they make no attempt to prevent boys and girls from playing together. Neither boys nor girls are required to wear clothes, except at school. Opportunities are unlimited for learning, since youngsters rarely are excluded from listening to a conversation on any subject. Furthermore, their observations include seeing animals copulate. Because their child may at this age attempt to watch them having sexual intercourse, parents remove him from the bedroom. They fear the child will embarrass them by interrupting them or by reporting in public what he has seen. Parents say they regard five- to eight-year-old children as relatively sexless. Yet boys play with their penises in public with impunity, while girls would be severely chastised if they touch their own genitals.

At the same time the five- or six-year-old is moved from his small bed or mat to another room, he may be yielding his space to a younger sibling who has been sleeping in the same bed with his parents. The location of the new sleeping place depends on the layout of the house. In a small dwelling, older children of different sexes occupy the same room, but have different beds. This separation is the earliest overt recognition by parents that children might attempt to have sexual intercourse. If the house does not contain space for an extra bedroom, the children will sleep in the room used for receiving guests and for eating. Sleeping in the midst of noise and activity is a common experience for children since they accompany their parents on social visits and to all-night wakes.

Games and Storytelling   Besides the play that imitates practical activities, children participate in organized games during this age-period. Of the large number and variety of games, those specifically for either boys or girls generally entail manual skills. Boys, for example, have spinning tops made of small snail shells. In one game, each player must adroitly spin his shell to win by knocking an opponent's top out of a hollow scooped in the ground. Wrestling is another game for boys only, though girls will wrestle in anger if provoked. Boys also play a variety of tag in which one of them imitates an *owu* dancer and chases the others. Sometimes the person who is "it" wears a toy mask. Girls, on the other hand, play a game that takes some precision in hopping from one foot to the other while repeating standard phrases rapidly. Another favorite preoccupation of children is storytelling. Before a child reaches his eighth year he can make up a story by fitting together short episodes from tales he has heard from adults or older children. The discontinuity of narrative and the misuse of words greatly amuse adults, since the errors indicate that children lack an understanding of what they are repeating.

VALUES

A child internalizes prescribed modes of behavior by exposure to a wide range of experiences in association with parents at home and playmates in his section. By the end of this age-period he has hardly acquired all the values of Ijaw culture, nor. can he know the implications of those he has learned, but his behavior and his verbal responses make plain that the process has well begun.

Parents encourage their children to aid others, but they would not punish them for refusing. The first response of a child to a question of whether he would help someone of his own age is generally a categorical affirmative. When the question is qualified with the proviso that the hypothetical child had never helped him, then the customary answer is changed to a negative reaction. Slightly older children, in the upper portion of the age bracket under discussion, view the situation somewhat differently. They say they would help, whether the older child aided them previously or not, because he might eventually return the favor. Both emphasize reciprocity, indicating that children learn at this early age the Ijaw value on helping others in order to receive similar treatment.

The value placed on reciprocity comes into play in other ways. A child is expected to share his food not only with his siblings, but with any visitor. Boys and girls reflect this value by stating that the best thing they could do for their friends is to invite them to share a meal. If a child, eating with his siblings or friends, refuses to share or takes too large a portion, his mother will rebuke him and take his food away. Should the child refuse to share because his previous invitations had not been reciprocated, his mother will not interfere or correct him.

Adults place great emphasis on working, and intertwine it with another value, obedience to parents and elders. A child is thought to be good if he obeys and carries out his assignments. A bad child ignores commands and neglects his tasks. Mothers make little distinction in this respect between an offspring who sweeps or washes the dishes quickly, efficiently, and without grumbling and one who works slowly, since both are obeying her instructions. This consideration of what constitutes a well-behaved child is evident in parental descriptions of a hypothetically bad child. His first credential is his refusal to do household tasks or to run errands. Responses from children indicate that they are acquiring these values by the time they are six or seven years old. Asked about the expectations of their parents, they reply that a good child is one who applies himself to whatever work his parents ask of him.

The value placed on obedience, like that on aid, is qualified by the importance of reciprocity, as illustrated in the following:

> Odeyo tells her five-year-old son to bring in the clothes drying outside because it is beginning to rain. Usako refuses, saying that she had earlier refused to give him a knife he wanted to play with. She laughs and brings in the clothes herself.

Mothers foster this type of response by threatening not to cook or buy clothing for their children if their instructions are not followed.

By the time children are five they can distinguish different forms of behavior toward their elders. To "bend the knee" to an older person as a form of etiquette is one thing, but whether the child will obey him is quite another matter and depends on their relationship. If the adult is in a position to punish him, whether he be a relative or parental surrogate, the child will usually obey. If a grown person, like his mother's co-wife, would not punish him but does many things for him, the child may also comply. On the other hand, a child usually refuses to obey an adult who neither helps nor can punish him.

Overt aggression, as a value, receives little encouragement among the Ijaw, but the principle of retaliation is inculcated in children. By forcing a boy or girl to fight back if a playmate attacks, parents often find their children become more aggressive than they wish and complain that their progeny fight too much, insulting one another at the least provocation. If one should accidentally throw dirt on another, inadvertently blink his eye at him—an insulting act when intentional—or if a boy tries too often to act the leader in a game or does not play the game well enough, an exchange of insults may quickly follow. These competitive exercises approach adult standards in vocal intensity and varieties of expression. Since parents adjure excessive violence, they intervene when a quarrel becomes a wrestling match or the argument persists after one opponent has fallen.

Adults react differently should their child fight someone older or younger than himself. A mother consoles her child if he comes home crying from a fight with an older child. Unless she is moved by the passion of the moment, however, she is careful not to strike her child's adversary and only threatens to tell his parents. Otherwise, she would extend the chain of involvement to his parents and create a serious quarrel. Conversely, parents discovering that their own child has beaten one his junior, first point out that he would suffer if this happened to him and then flog him if he persists.

To insult an adult, or fight with him, is considered gross impoliteness in view of the Ijaw belief that those older than oneself should be respected and obeyed. A high incidence of conflicts between children and their mothers illustrates the problem children in this age-period and the next have in separating the two values of respect and retaliation. Mothers relate that their offspring insult them as though they are age-mates or co-wives, and strike them with sticks or hard pieces of mud. One woman claims she has to be careful not to turn her back to her five-year-old son when he is angry for fear he will cut her with a knife. Our observations confirm that these statements are not exaggerations. The difficulty children experience in choosing between approved modes of behavior may be intensified by the practice of mothers usually treating infantile displays of aggression very lightly. After exchanging blows or throwing mud back at the child, they laugh and drop the matter unless repeatedly provoked.

> Obe is quarreling with another boy and his mother tells him to stop. He becomes annoyed and hits her. She tries to push him away. He attempts to bite her. She becomes angry when he spits at her and then she beats him.

Another difficulty in striking a balance between the principle of retaliation and the principle of respect is the inherent contradiction of the two. Mothers inflict restrictions and punishments that to a child must sometimes seem like acts of aggression and, therefore, require retaliation. At the same time, mothers give rewards and convey approbation. Children were never seen to strike their fathers, who play a minor role in punishing them.

The Ijaw pride themselves on their honesty, and conversely, consider stealing to be shameful and dangerous. Adults reason that stealing is a particularly heinous crime because the thief involves his family as well as himself. Not only does he bring shame to his kinsmen, he threatens their lives should the owner of the stolen property invoke an *oru* against the thief. Parents feel strongly enough about stealing to say they would kill a child not able to be cured of thieving. The emphasis on this value seems to have the desired effect. In Ebiama Christians, who theoretically cease to believe in the power of the *orumo*, or persons in a position to steal from Europeans with the knowledge that no *oru* would be invoked, show the same propensity for honesty.

Parents of children younger than five have no problem with their progeny stealing because infants cannot enter a house without being observed by those assigned to care for them. As soon as a child is capable of taking food himself, however, his mother begins to warn him not to take it without permission. A child taking food from his own home cannot be seriously accused of stealing, but parents choose precisely this matter of obtaining food without permission to train their children not to steal. From the age of five onward, to remove edibles, even in one's own home, incurs severe penalties.

Withholding or offering food are important techniques used to inculcate several different behavioral and ideational traits throughout childhood. An infant is fed, for the most part on demand, first by his mother and later by the surrogate caring for him. A five- to eight-year-old is more independent but he must come to coordinate his demands with his mother's schedule of activities. If she plans to be away from the village during the day, she leaves prepared food for him or foods which he can easily roast, such as dried fish and plantain. She instructs him not to touch the other food in the house since she plans to use it for the evening meal. Mothers are usually generous in the amount they leave, but children often quickly devour it. Being accustomed to eating whenever hungry, they find it difficult to ration what they have until their mothers return from their work. Despite the punishment that invariably follows, most children succumb to the temptation to pilfer food or to find means of obtaining some elsewhere.

Rewards and Punishments Parental attitudes toward good or bad behavior of children between the age of five and eight are reflected in the types of rewards given to children performing tasks well. Some mothers state they do nothing to reward their sons or daughters because, in the first place, they have nothing to give them and secondly, that not scolding them should be reward enough. Nonetheless, most mothers respond positively to good behavior, saying that they "love" a child or "are happy with him." Instead of showing physical affection, they award a penny, a cloth, or extra food, or praise and thank him. They repeat that he can expect his clothing, food, or school fees to be provided in the future. While parents say they praise a preadolescent, they qualify the statement by adding that they praise him in his absence, expecting that their comments will eventually reach him. Ijaw believe direct praise turns the head of the child, causing him to become proud and to refuse to work. To say "thank you," adults claim, is sufficient. Children agree by saying they expect nothing from their parents for proper behavior.

Parents more easily describe a bad child than a good one. He wets his bed, steals, disobeys, refuses to perform household tasks, or insults his elders. Severe punishments await any boy or girl falling into this category. These include: withholding food, rubbing pepper into cuts purposely made on the face and body, and holding the culprit near the fire to increase the pain, rubbing pepper or mentholated ointment into the eyes and genitals, flogging, insults and public ridicule. Withholding food is thought by adults to be the worst of these because there is no escape from hunger, whereas pepper can quickly be washed off.

The type of disciplinary measure a parent chooses depends on whether the child has ignored previous warnings for committing an offense, his age and size, the person outside the family he has offended, or more obliquely, on how the parent feels that day. Should a child believe his parent is beating him unjustly, he can try to obtain protection, most often from the other parent or from older relatives living nearby. A culprit knows, however, that if he has done something wrong, his relatives will not protect him. Abuse and ridicule are the most customary punishments, but beatings are occasionally severe, as evidenced by the bruises children display. A woman hits her child with a stick, rarely her hand, and directs blows to any part of his body, including the face.

Should refusing food be the punishment, it is withheld only for a few hours or at most until the evening meal, never for an entire day or night. A mother relents, women say, because she remembers how unhappy she herself was at this treatment during her own childhood and therefore empathizes with the child. Two other considerations temper her anger. Her husband may intervene or the child's cries may bring neighbors, usually relatives. If a child runs to another house for protection, his mother could be taunted for trying to starve her offspring or make him ill.

To make children behave or to stop them from crying, parents no longer threaten to call animals and *owumǫ,* earlier used to frighten them, since boys and girls of this age-period have come to realize that they are harmless. It will be recalled that a child is never threatened by what is believed by parents to be truly dangerous: the dead, *orumǫ* and *diriguǫyou.* Recalcitrants are promised the various punishments mentioned above or that the matter will be referred to their fathers, although in practice women rarely carry out the latter threat.

Mothers take primary responsibility for discipline, but in principle anyone concerned with a child's welfare, that is, any of his close kin, can chastise him. As in the previous age-period, women say they welcome this assistance, even from co-wives, but a child's parents are usually the only ones who punish him corporally. Even those relatives with a right to strike a child prefer to report his delinquency to the mother and let her decide what to do. In this way they are no different from non-relatives in the village, in that everyone feels free to speak to a parent whose child has misbehaved. Boys and girls thus quickly learn the wisdom behind Ijaw proverbs, such as, "whatever you do in the bush or water will come out." One boy expressed this viewpoint by saying he never lied to his parents about his malefactions because someone was bound to have seen him and would tell them.

RELIGION

During this age-period a child has only slight and often incorrect knowledge of the nonhuman beings that dominate the adult conception of the world. He knows some of the more common terms for them, such as *oru* and *duwoiyou,* and will fear them, even though adults try not to frighten infants with *oru* or the dead, nor threaten to invoke them to punish a delinquent. Despite this absence of explicit references, juveniles have many opportunities to observe events that involve *orumǫ* and *duwoiyou,* and to consider the attitudes of their elders toward them.

Boys and girls claim they are more afraid of the dead and of animals of the bush than of any other elements in the cultural milieu. They, and adults as well, say that ghosts kill a person by striking him with clubs. Because *duwoiyou* are often encountered in the forest, children believe they normally live there rather than, as adults believe, in the town of the dead. Many boys and girls recall the great fear they had on nights someone died in the village, despite the absence of an adult belief or ritual during the funeral that would indicate *duwoiyou* are more dangerous immediately after death than later.

At the various types of funerals mentioned earlier, the focus of attention rests on the ability of the deceased to reveal the reasons for death by moving the *obębę.* The explanation usually includes references to the power of the *orumǫ* and ancestors to kill. Children rarely participate actively in funerals, with one exception. A boy or girl may be chosen to act as the *kǫnu tǫbǫu* (first born child) at a funeral. The person selected for this role wears special dress and initiates certain dances. Since the *kǫnu tǫbǫu* literally represents the deceased, he is very much the center of activities and receives the same deference as would be shown the person who died. Old people, younger than the deceased, "bend the knee" as a sign of respect while greeting or taking drink from the *kǫnu tobǫu* during the funeral proceedings.

An experience some children have, could heighten fear of the *orumọ*, is participation in an extremely painful rite for a parent who has been made ill by an *oru*. As part of the cure, a herbal mixture is squeezed into the eyes of both parent and child. At the same time children are acquiring fear of *orumọ*, they also become acquainted with their potential benevolence. On the simplest level, their power is dramatized by the frequent presentations of food made in the cult-houses. A small amount is set aside for the *orumọ* and later given to the children; offerings of palm wine or gin alone are also shared with all the children present.

Yet another signification of *orumọ* derives from the play associated with them on certain occasions. A ritual enjoyed by younger people takes place when a diviner determines that a forest *oru* is causing the delay of a birth. This calls for a propitiatory rite called *okoka pogholo* (a hole made by grubs). On one occasion we observed the rite for a woman well past the predicted time of delivery:

> Yenge [very swollen from pregnancy] sits on the ground with her feet in a hollow section of a rotten log especially brought to the village for the ceremony. A large crowd has gathered to watch. Dabo is in charge. He selects fourteen children at random from between the ages of five and ten to participate, gives each a long, strong stalk of a weed and instructs them on how to use it. The participants stand in front of the log and strike their sticks on the ground while Dabo implores the forest deities to release the unborn infant. [One boy, who had previously participated in this type of ceremony, tells a younger child not to pound his stalk too much because it will soften the end.] On cue from Dabo, the youngsters run by the seated woman and try to strike her stomach with the stalks. Dabo tries to ward off some of the blows, but enough land to hurt Yenge. The children circle around repeatedly and attempt to hit her before they are told to run behind nearby buildings. Yenge then escapes.

The children's participation in this ceremony raises difficult problems in interpreting what it means to them. Adults and the young participants themselves are inarticulate about the reasons for their actions. Presumably, they are included because of the belief discussed previously that children have the power to communicate with the unborn.

In their games juveniles reenact parts of what they observe at ceremonies, emphasizing again that certain rituals, in the proper context, can be treated lightly and without awe. Boys of this age play at being *owumọ* in a more elaborate fashion than described for the previous age-period. Adult masquerade dances, it will be recalled, are performed by Christians purely for entertainment at Christmas time, by anyone at funerals, and by worshippers of an *owu* as a sacred rite. In playing *owu*, boys dress one of themselves by placing a cloth over his face and a small carved *owu* (or a stick to represent it) on his head. Sometimes the costume is more elaborate, including a long cloth trailing behind to act as a "tail." Unlike adult performers, children do not wear leg rattles or bells, nor dance, and there is no drumming. A small stick serves as a machete. The object of the game is for the *owu* dancer to whip the other boys, who taunt him as he tries to catch them. Asked why the smallest boy is always chosen to be the *owu* dancer, one youth explained that picking the slowest runner presumes the others will not be flogged too often. If an older boy were allowed to be *owu*, he could beat the younger ones and they would not play again. Adults believe the game prepares the youths for eventual

Ceremony performed for pregnant woman whose delivery is divined as being delayed by forest spirits.

participation in the actual *owu* dance and therefore encourage the imitation to the point of carving play-masks for them.

Children in this age-period are indifferent to the *diriguǫyou*, whose powers to injure others secretly are feared in the adult world as much as that of *orumǫ* and *duwoiyou*. Preadolescents have a number of opportunities to learn about sorcery, as when they observe the *obębę* being asked at funerals whether the deceased was an evil person (*diriguǫkęmę*). Stories told by adults often refer to sorcerers, and the habit of taking a drink before handing it to another person is a constant visual reminder of the danger of poisoning for which only *diriguǫyou* are responsible. Nonetheless, the children seem to have little comprehension of the danger involved.

Their innocence is particularly evident in the replies they give to questions about causes and cures of illnesses. Even those as young as five years old know something about simple herbal remedies for wounds and claim they can apply these themselves. Furthermore, all informants remember having had an ailment of one sort or another, but not one boy or girl in the five to eight age range mention poison as a cause. According to them, their sicknesses came from Wǫnyinghi, a fall, or constipation. A few had no idea of how their illnesses originated. Obviously children are not asked to diagnose their own ailments; usually they hear their parents or diviners discuss the nature of their infirmity and its cause. We assume that preadolescents, unlike adults, ignore the malevolence of *diriguǫyou* because their own illnesses were not severe enough to have been caused by sorcerers. Another explanation can be seen in the ways adults react to children's interpretations. When a child names *orumǫ* and *duwoiyou* as the sources of unexplainable noises and movements at night or in the forest, he is the object of solicitude from his parents and neighbors, who coddle him and attentively listen to him. But a child claiming to have been poisoned would be making an accusation that "someone," a *diriguǫkęmę*, has poisoned him. Once someone is suspected, then the question is, who? The very question engenders bad feelings and rumors begin to spread. If, indeed, someone were accused, he could take the person making the accusation and his guardian to court for defamation of character. Parents are therefore unlikely to encourage references to poisoning.

CIRCUMCISION

At no other time is the absence of formal Ijaw institutions for imparting cultural ideals more evident than during circumcision, which in many African societies provides an opportunity for the inculcation of traditional lore and modes of behavior. In its traditional place in the life cycle, circumcision itself could be said to be somehow symbolic of this age-period, as the "age of transition" between infancy and adulthood. As noted previously, in Ebiama the time of the operation was changed from the age of five or older to early infancy without apparent loss to the indigenous pattern of enculturation. This change does not, however, mitigate its importance. A male must be circumcised if he is to participate in adult life.

Several men in their thirties remember the occasion of their circumcision, which they estimate took place when they were about eight years old. Without warning, their fathers sent them to the river to "cool" their blood. Bathing, men believe, limits the possibility of hemorrhage. On returning, several men seized them and held them down on a bed of plantain leaves. They were allowed to cry out as much as they wanted during the operation. Immediately after the foreskin was detached, their parents gave them gifts, including fish to eat, to halt their crying. Several weeks later, after the wound had healed, beads—of the type worn by an infant after his first tooth erupts, by a person acting as a *kǫnu tǫbǫu,* and by wrestlers—were placed around their necks and waists, and their heads were shaved.

Boys of this age-period still uncircumcised because of illness or the like are threatened with the operation to induce them to behave, and therefore they fear it. Otherwise, boys deny any knowledge of its significance. In the conception of mature Ijaw, it is incomprehensible to be both an adult and uncircumcised since it is a prerequisite to marriage and attendance at ceremonies in the cult-houses.

In summary, between the ages of five and eight, girls have started-to practice the occupations they will perform later, and both boys and girls are gradually acquiring responsibility in their households. The distinction between good and bad behavior is introduced, and, coincidentally, Ijaw believe the soul has now lost the extraordinary power of its infancy. Knowledge of values remains limited and behavior appears to be based more on the principle of avoiding discomfort than on any appreciation of basic cultural values. Nevertheless, the five to eight age-period has molded the enculturative base for becoming an Ijaw. In the next chapter we shall see how the child begins not only to better understand his cultural world, but to participate in it as a somewhat more active member of his society.

6/Childhood from nine to thirteen: the age of responsibility

AS THE IJAW CHILD reaches about his ninth year he assumes new responsibilities. He watches over his younger siblings or junior kinsmen, taking care of all their needs during the day and being held accountable should they hurt themselves. He begins to make a significant economic contribution to his household. With the fulfillment of these obligations he all but completes the shift from being wholly dependent on others to having others dependent on him.

Girls contribute more to the household than boys at this time. Their steadily increasing proficiency in producing food and in discharging household tasks means that by the time they are thirteen they are prepared to assume the responsibilities of marriage. In the case of boys, not until the next age-period will they be mature enough to work in ways that will permit them to become productive members of their society.

This phase can be viewed as a "threshold to adulthood"[1] because it includes much more participation in adult life than assuming economic responsibilities alone. Boys and girls expand their knowledge of their environment by traveling to other villages and even to cities on the mainland. They show evidence of having deepened their view of the cultural world by telling stories with an understanding of their content, rather than merely imitating what they have heard. Furthermore, they are able to explain or rationalize some of their own behavior. Recognition of approaching maturity is most clearly seen in the emphasis adults and older children place on ridicule as a method of rebuking them. Although parents still mete out physical punishment to ensure conformity, children are expected to distinguish right from wrong and to feel ashamed for bad behavior.

This borderline period also includes certain characteristics of maturation that are prerequisite for attaining the status of an adult. Boys and girls are now strong enough to carry, wash, and protect their wards. They can handle themselves in canoes well enough to take the stern position, thereby allowing them to travel by themselves. Through earlier practice they have become dextrous in manual skills associated with household tasks, weaving, and building bird traps. The girls, reaching puberty, wear cloths about their waists at all times, and earlier play-groups now evolve into associations made up exclusively of either boys or girls.

These general characteristics mark off the children of nine to thirteen from those

---

[1] This phrase is used by Read (1959) to describe a later stage, adolescence, in Ngoni childhood.

younger and older. From an overall view, a child enculturating to Ijaw culture is like a roll of film in that the following sequence has taken place up to this point: first, from birth to four years old the film is exposed. Then, from five to eight the negative takes shape as the boy or girl reflects Ijaw life, but with little of the texture that comes from the personal expression of cultural meaning. Finally, from nine to thirteen the negative is contact printed and the photograph of an enculturated Ijaw begins to appear. Each child is an individual photograph, though the similarities among them are greater than the differences. The uncertain results of the enculturative process can be included in this analogy, for this age-period, like a roll of film, is characterized by a number of "poor exposures," unsocialized children whose parents have not yet been able to shape them into the Ijaw mold of being obedient, hard working, and honest.

HOUSEHOLD AND ECONOMIC ACTIVITIES

A child younger than nine has occasionally been charged with caring for an infant, but the significant requirement for the present age-period is that he demonstrates a sense of responsibility. A mother feels he can be trusted not to run away as soon as she leaves for her farm. She believes he will prevent the toddler from going near the fireplace and the river, and from cutting himself with a knife. She is also confident he will not have a fit of anger and physically harm his ward. Beyond these minimal requirements, the preadolescent should be counted on to respond whenever the infant in his care cries, and to keep him happy and satisfied by playing with him.

Since the internalization of a sense of responsibility begins at the age of seven, most children accept their duties now without demur, particularly since they can continue to devote most of their time to play. Rarely does a boy or girl reach the end of this age-period without having had some experience caring for an infant.

The role of nurse, as one who cares for a younger sibling may be called, imposes the greatest responsibility a juvenile must assume, but he is also liable for the care of his own person and for performing certain household and economic tasks. These have been described to some extent for the previous age-period, but a subtle difference is to be noted in the way adults now emphasize responsibility, and the corresponding reactions of the children. Parents expect a child of five to eight years of age to be obedient and to perform whatever task is set for him. Yet they assume he will not perform it without being told each time to do so, even when the activity is repetitive, like the daily sweeping of the floor, and the response of a boy or girl appears to be primarily motivated by the desire to please his parents and escape punishment. At about age nine, parents fully anticipate that their offspring will discharge their obligations without constantly being reminded. The child, as far as he verbalizes his responses, believes he should perform his tasks not only to avoid punishment—though this is still important for assuring proper behavior—but because he wants to assist his mother, who in return helps him.

By nine years of age, he has already learned to bathe himself, wash his own

Carrying a younger sibling.

Washing him.

Guarding him at the farm (left)
while mother works (right).

Playing with him.

clothes, and make his own toilet. Although the element of play in bathing persists, and makes going to the river at least twice a day during the dry season an enjoyable habit, he now recognizes the importance of cleanliness to avoid insults from adults and playmates. This generalized concept of cleanliness is extended to many of his other habits: his clothes must be clean for the same reason as his body. He knows he should use his left hand to wash his anus because that hand is "unclean," and therefore he must also not touch food with it.

In the house the preadolescent sweeps the floor, carries water, and washes plates. He can carry water in a bucket, transporting the container on his head. Cooking is the one household task in which the mother continues to give daily instruction. A girl becomes fairly accomplished at cooking by this time and can prepare a meal for the entire household. Nonetheless, a woman expecting to return from the forest too late to prepare the evening meal herself must still tell her daughter what food to place on the fire. Usually the mother cooks the food and her son or daughter helps by peeling vegetables and performing the arduous task of beating cassava. A boy, too, must be able to cook for at least himself and those whom he guards, since parents do not yet insist on fully adult patterns in the sexual division of labor. This means that girls' tasks, such as farming, will be their future responsibilities, whereas boys work simply to assist their mothers. At twelve or thirteen, a girl is given her own farm by a parent or kinsman, but her mother must still help her with the clearing, even though the plot is usually very small. Food from these farms, unlike the products of play-farms, is used in feeding the family. Girls occasionally grow enough cocoyams and sugar cane to sell and may keep the money for themselves.

In weaving mats and fishing baskets, a thirteen-year-old girl gathers the bamboo that she needs from the forest. She must still depend on her mother for raffia, which is more difficult to obtain. Prior to the season for fishing, she can weave up to sixty traps, most of which she gives to her mother. If a woman catches many fish and has a surplus to sell, she usually purchases a gift of clothes for her daughter to indicate appreciation for her assistance. A preadolescent keeps some of the traps for her own fishing and, now that she has learned to steer a canoe, fishes with line and hooks on the river each evening, usually with a girl her own age or younger to help paddle. Parents encourage their daughters to fish and thank them warmly if they return with a catch.

Fishing provides the principal way for boys to contribute to household needs. They follow the same pattern of fishing as their sisters and turn over large fish to their mothers. Boys and girls whose parents take them on fishing expeditions to the mangrove swamps during the school holidays or to more distant fishing spots for several years at a time, have the opportunity to become indispensable helpers.

Girls earn a little money by trading and by assisting some relative other than their fathers in distilling gin. In the first instance, a strong girl might be asked to go along on a trading trip, usually with one of her relatives, to paddle and cook. Her parents or kinsmen lend her some money to buy foodstuffs at the market and on returning to Ebiama she sells what she has brought home, repays the loan, and keeps the profit. In the second instance, a distiller would give a girl a few shillings or a cloth for tending the fires and seeing to it that the gin is processed correctly.

Weaving a sleeping mat.

If the distiller is her father, instead of paying her, he gives her a small gift after she has been particularly helpful.

Unlike the girls, boys of this age-period do not trade, either from lack of opportunity and interest or because school keeps them busy. They earn money by helping a gin distiller and by making thatch mats for roofing, though parents or older kinsmen must collect the palm leaves for them. Thatch mats offer a good way to earn money because they are required for the annual roof repairs. Boys become most proficient and spend much of their time making and setting bird traps. This effort brings them no money and the birds are not eaten. The number snared appears to be very small and in no way proportionate to the time devoted to the production of the traps. This interest in bird traps emphasizes the essential difference between the preoccupations of the sexes during their youth. The boys concentrate on an activity that produces little gain and has no direct replica in the adult world. Girls practice the tasks of women by spending most of their working time on weaving, fishing, or farming and receive material rewards. Although the boys help gin distillers, they only tend the fires which is essentially the work of women.

Not all boys' activites are consistent with the observation just made. One of the best examples of their preparing to take their place as adults in the indigenous scheme of production can be found in the task of manufacturing palm oil. Between the ages of five and eight a boy will have begun to help his parents by sorting nuts after the bunches are brought to the village. Later, he begins to follow palm fruit collectors to the forest to gather the nuts that are shaken loose as the men cut down the palm bunches. The Ijaw regard this work as the first step in learning the traditional occupation for men. The boy gives the fruit he collects to his mother, who uses them in her cooking, or he processes them himself. Preadolescents are not strong enough to attempt to climb a palm tree, but a few will have gone up the less hazardous coconut trees. Fishing is another exception. Boys begin to imitate the fishing techniques used by men, but as we have noted, few men choose to fish full time.

The basic motivations for learning adult skills can be summarized as follows: First, as in the previous age-period, the preadolescent performs his tasks to please his parents and because he believes a good child is one who works. Second, children emphatically say they do certain things to obtain rewards. More than any other single item children say they desire money to buy food or clothes for themselves. This suggests that the interest of children in personal possessions is a complementary value to that of respecting the rights of others. Parents believe that a child who prizes the food or clothing purchased with his own money will be hesitant to take what belongs to others.

Acquiring a sense of responsibility, whether it be epitomized by caring for an infant or in personal care and productive tasks, is a combination of maturation and the internalization of values. The latter appears to be initially based on behavior conditioned by the child's expectation of punishment should he act irresponsibly. Before discussing more fully the role of punishment in learning, and its more infrequent counterpart, reward, mention should be made of another attitude attached to work which at first seems at odds with adult values.

The majority of children claim they would prefer to work in groups rather than by themselves. Adults, it will be recalled, choose to work alone. Men give this as a reason for wishing to distill gin rather than collect palm fruits. This discontinuity in preference can partially be explained by the reaction of children to a hypothetical situation in which they have the choice of working alone or with others. They immediately assume the place of work to be the forest and explain their preference for working with others by saying that they will have assistance if any strange being is encountered or if they hurt themselves. In actual practice, preadolescents keep each other company while working individually at their tasks, whether play-farming or making bird traps, unless one is teaching another.

METHODS OF TEACHING

Of the methods used by parents to motivate their young to learn techniques and values, we find, as at younger ages, that punishment far outweighs reward. Adults believe a nine- to thirteen-year-old should perform tasks and assume responsibilities as a natural part of growing up. His assistance, therefore, receives no more acknowledgment than that given to a grown-up. Adult relatives are expected to help each other without remuneration, except for the food provided during the work. Men occasionally give small gifts to their wives for aiding them, but paid labor even between unrelated individuals is a post-British innovation. All assistance in earlier times was repaid in kind. Extending these precepts to children over the age of nine means that a youth should go about his household duties and care for a ward without expecting more than a word of thanks and his meals.

This pattern of de-emphasizing rewards is similar to the one for younger children, except for a difference in connotation. The "thank you" to a younger child is meant to be a source of encouragement in his effort to perform a task. The appreciation expressed to an older one would not be forthcoming unless he did indeed perform adequately. The preadolescent, then, is regarded as having left his infancy behind and he may now be praised directly without fear that this will make him too proud to continue assisting his parents.

Physical punishment also approaches the standards of adult behavior. On one occasion a woman struck her thirteen-year-old daughter on the head with a stick, giving her a severe wound, for refusing to tend the youngest infant in the household. Parents in their anger over an act of disobedience or neglect of responsibility will not look for a switch with which to beat the child, as they do with younger ones, but strike him with fists or an open hand as they would in fighting another adult.

Mothers continue to threaten to withhold food to emphasize the reciprocal nature of work. One who fails to do his share of work should not expect the other members of his family to provide food for him. Along with threats of this sort and with the promises of a whipping, parents mix a constant flow of derision that ranges from comments on a repulsive physical characteristic of the child to invidious comparisons with age-mates.

Nine to thirteen-year-olds respond to these punishments differently from younger children. An older child becomes adept at avoiding beatings by employing one of several avenues of escape open to him: lie, run out of the house, go to another grown-up for protection, fight back, send someone to ask forgiveness, or prepare to invoke a deity on behalf of his innocence. Each of these will be taken up in turn. From past experience, a preadolescent knows quite well that he will be punished whether he admits a misdemeanor or not, so he may make up a story. Sometimes running away is attempted without success by younger children, but preadolescents can often run more swiftly than their parents. If a youth misbehaves, he rarely attempts to go to another adult for protection, though he knows by this time which individuals will harbor him if he is being unjustly punished. Indeed, this is a significant step in the process of differentiating kinsmen from other adults. In unintentional instances of misbehavior, such as breaking a plate or losing an item of clothing or other property, a preadolescent tries to avoid his parents until they have time to calm down. He then asks one of his kinsmen to mediate by explaining the matter to them. The final means of avoiding a beating, that of swearing one's innocence, is used only in serious types of misbehavior and will be described later.

While all children misbehave at some time, there are a few children whose main motivation in shirking all duties seems to lie in the challenge of avoiding punishment. They appear to be incorrigibles, which will be more apparent in a description of antisocial behavior below. For now it suffices to say that fear of punishment, at least, has not appreciably helped children of this type to become responsible members of the community. Contrary to these exceptions, the behavior of most children reveals that they feel shame (*ozu ẹnini*) or, at least, that they are aware a show of contriteness is the quickest way to make parents forget their misbehavior. A child discovered to have wet his bed appears to be very embarrassed. Similarly, a child may refuse to accept food or some item he desires, such as ink for school, after his mother threatens not to give it to him or insults him for not helping in the house by saying, "But now you come to eat!" Parents believe this type of behavior indicates shame.

KINSHIP

A nine- to thirteen-year-old knows to whom he can run for protection and he also knows which kinsmen have the authority to beat and ridicule him. A preadolescent is quick to remind an adult who wishes to punish him that if they do not have a close relationship, his parents will take his side regardless of what he has done.

Besides distinguishing between relatives and nonrelatives, by the way in which they unequally offer assistance, protection, or inflict punishments, most boys and girls have become better acquainted with the rights and obligations of family members by having lived in the household of a relative at some time or by being helped more by one member of a kinship group than by another. They learn to differentiate between simple reciprocal obligations and established rights of specific kinsmen. They grasp, in other words, the normative connotations of kinship terms.

Although nearly half the children in Ebiama do not live with both their parents, boys of this age anticipate that after they marry they will reside in the village sections of their fathers. Boys who have never lived with their fathers explain their preference by saying, "It is good to live in the place of one's father." Their attitude appears to be influenced by visits to their fathers, who continually remind them of their rightful place of residence. From a practical point of view, children see that the maintenance of ties with both father and mother, and their respective kinsmen, provides them with what might be called a double line of defense. Feeling mistreated where he lives, whether he resides with his mother or father, a child can run to the section of the other parent. At any other time he may visit that part of the village for a meal or to play with children without any possibilty of his being sent away for not belonging. The few children preferring not to live in their paternal section are boys whose fathers are dead or continuously absent from the village.

Sometimes a question arises as to who should pay a child's school fees and buy his supplies. If the father refuses aid, the mother's brother, *yabę,* will be asked to pay these expenses. A child comes to recognize the importance of the *yabę* since he himself must ask for the school money.

Aside from using kinship terms in direct address for consanguines in ascending generations, a preadolescent refers to most of his other relatives by their personal names or by the all-inclusive term for kinsmen, *bonara* or *bonawei* (sister or brother). During this age-period he learns to distinguish terminologically between full and half-siblings. With his full or maternal half-siblings, *kęnę nyinmo,* he must help, share with, and protect those younger than himself, or he will be punished if an adult relative happens to observe him neglecting them. In turn a youth expects to receive these same considerations from siblings older than himself. Paternal half-siblings, *kęnę daubo,* continue to have a close relationship, participating in the

Young men wrestling.

same play-groups if they are of comparable age or teaching each other new activities. However, even though a youth helps his *kẹnẹ daubọ* to fight outsiders, within the household a *kẹnẹ nyinmọ* always comes first in cases requiring sides be taken in quarrelling, sharing, or giving assistance.

PLAY-GROUPS

Preadolescents play with children living nearby as well as with their siblings, but the activities of these play-groups differ in several ways from those of the previous age-period. In the first place, most of the children now must guard infants

Young men wrestling.

whom they carry on their backs or toddlers while they play. Secondly, nine to thirteen-year-olds are the informal leaders in games, singing the accompanying songs, giving instructions to the younger participants, and being corrected only occasionally by adolescents or adults. Most games are not imitative of any adult activity of practical value, as play-cooking was at a younger age, but are games per se, with their own rules and objectives. A partial exception is a game played only by boys in which a player swings a piece of plantain stalk around his head on a long rope while the others, grouped in a circle about him, try to spear the moving stalk with sharp bamboo slivers. Each participant drops out as he succeeds. The last one remaining has his hand beaten with their slivers by the other players. A variation of this sport employs a rolling disc as the target. The obvious objective of both, which the Ijaw recognize, is to train the youth for spear fishing, an activity attempted by boys in the next age-period.

Telling stories is a favorite pastime of the children in the evenings or while they work at a sedentary task, such as weaving, during the day. Smaller children, we saw, try to recite tales, but they cannot match the knowledge of the older boys and girls. All the tales are learned from other children or adults and the story-telling sessions closely imitate the pattern of adult gatherings. On a warm evening about a dozen children gather on a verandah on which the adult members of the household are also sitting and chatting. One of the youths faces the others and begins with "Egberiyo!" (story), to which the audience replies, "Ya!" He continues, "Once it happened in Edo (Benin) that . . .," one of the several conventional openings. Many times during the course of the tale the storyteller or someone in the audience shouts "Egberiyo!" and the listeners respond in unison with "Ya!" to indicate they are still alert.

The stories themselves are told as "true" narratives. The themes often involve fantastic accounts of sorcerers, of fights between co-wives, or of sibling antagonisms. They follow the usual practice of having the number three continually represented, either by repeating a part of the tale over three times, having three characters involved in the plot, or having the hero undergo three ordeals or the like before the end. The number seven recurs within the context of the tale almost as often. As with the association between numbers and the sexes, Ijaw offer no explanation for why these numbers appear so frequently here and elsewhere in their culture. Another typical characteristic of stories containing malevolent characters is for the storyteller to pose the question:

"Which character is guilty?"

The answer always is the first one who acted wrongly. The story noted earlier of a son killing his mother for her failure to protect him is an example of this type.

Although the narrator speaks as quickly as possible and without hesitation, he can take an hour to finish, a moderate length of time for an Ijaw story. At the end the speaker recounts that he heard the story from a particular person, thereby sharing the responsibility for the truth of its contents, and concludes:

"Egberifa!" (story finished).

The audience, including the adults, rejoin with an appreciative:

"Ya!"

Should another child choose to tell a tale, or be asked to do so, the session continues for several more hours.

Ijaw tell stories primarily to entertain. If stories succeed in being didactic as well, this is a by-product rather than an expressed aim. A child enhances his reputation as an entertainer by skillfully imitating the stylistic forms of narration. A preadolescent able to tell a story well or to listen attentively indicates that he has internalized some of its inherent ideas, whether it be about sorcerers or quarrelling between co-wives.

Male and Female Roles   Except for storytelling sessions, which draw all children living in the nearby area together, those aged nine to thirteen tend to have their play-groups divided by sex. Mothers emphatically point to this period of the life cycle as the time girls should "know themselves" and be careful not to compromise themselves with boys. As her first pubic hairs appear, a girl begins to wear a cloth around her waist and never again goes completely nude in public. During her baths at the waterside she keeps on her cloth until the water is above her waist. Parents and girls alike agree that it is bad for a young girl to have sexual intercourse before marriage, and should a man suspect his daughter of having had sexual relations or of contemplating them, he will beat her severely, whether his accusation can be proved or not. It is permissible, however, for girls of this age to refer to rules of etiquette associated with the sexual act in stories they repeat or in their songs, such as the following verse: "A man deceived me last night. He had sex without paying. Wǫnyinghi should punish him."

Fear of punishment only partly explains why a girl avoids private contact with boys and acts annoyed if one of them tries to touch her. In the past, supposedly, there was less prohibition on touching young girls' breasts. According to elderly Ijaw, this pattern changed because sorcery has increased and the girls fear "bad medicine" might be communicated to them by this kind of contact. Girls also avoid playing with boys to avoid initiating gossip about themselves. One twelve-year-old girl explained that she refused to attend school because adults in the community referred to all schoolgirls in a derogatory manner after a few of them had become pregnant. Nonetheless, a bad reputation gained from having premarital sexual intercourse will not in itself prevent a girl from marrying.

The prohibitions placed upon boys are somewhat different. Since girls of this age are supposed to refrain from having sexual intercourse, it follows that abstinence is forced on the boys, who are ignored by older girls. Parents say that as long as a boy has sex with a consenting unmarried woman, they would have no objection. If a boy cannot make an "arrangement" and tries to take a girl without her permission, he would be punished by his parents. There is no Ijaw equivalent to the English "rape." Assuming adultery is not at issue, no penalties are incurred when a girl or woman is forced to have sexual intercourse. Adults recall one instance of several preadolescents trying to force an eight-year-old girl to have sexual relations, but they were stopped and beaten by a male relative of the girl. This occasion illustrates the importance of a value described previously. The fathers of the boys would ordinarily have beaten their sons for attacking the girl. In this instance, however, since the man protecting the girl was unrelated to any of the

Girls playing.

Young women stringing beads that they will wear around their hips to make themselves look more attractive.

boys and not in a position to punish them without permission of their parents, the men vigorously defended their sons in the ensuing arguments.

Except at school, preadolescent boys still wear no clothing. Whereas girls this age paddle across the river to defecate in privacy, boys follow the pattern of men, who generally expose themselves more in public than women do, and defecate at the village waterside and bathe without a cloth. Unlike the men, boys continue to hold and pull their penises in public, but adults now tease them for doing so by saying they are acting like young children. Parents neither encourage nor reprimand their sons for masturbating in private. This again is in contrast to girls who, as we have said, should never expose their genitals and certainly not masturbate. Boys believe, or pretend to believe, girls do and taunt them with derisive comments, such as: "An unmarried girl could not find a lover, so she used roasted plantain." These sayings are used in songs or in other forms of indirect ridicule because the mention of personal names would instigate fights.

Members of this age-period become aware of the permanent associational groupings of age-mates (*zi ogbo*). Preadolescents come to know their age-mates from references made to them by their mothers and by the emphasis placed on age differential in patterns of respect and of retaliation in fights. The children learn that age-mates have a joking relationship that allows them freely to abuse one another. They are also aware that adult *zi ogbo* eat together occasionally, but since none of the boys is old enough to hunt for large animals, they obviously cannot follow this practice.

SOCIAL CONTROL

Within the context of kinship groups and associations, the preadolescent learns patterns of respect, control of aggression, and the consequences of antisocial behavior. His parents and schoolteachers represent the main figures of authority, but the reasons he puts forward for respecting them hint that he has only partially internalized the adult rationale for respect. A nine- to thirteen-year-old claims that he refrains from insulting older people because they sometimes help him or are stronger than he and would win in a fight. It is only later that respect for age is made articulate.

These preadolescent responses accurately reflect the general attitude toward aggression and its control. All Ijaw are unanimous in their opinion that one should retaliate against injury inflicted by a peer. Yet, as an individual grows older, he takes every opportunity to avoid fights, particularly those in which the outcome is in doubt. Peers who frequently quarrel are avoided, and according to the boys and girls themselves, one of the worst things a youth can do is fight with his friends. The displays of aggression also become much more structured for preadolescents than for younger juveniles. The former refuse to return an insult to someone older than themselves until they have been abused three times, and even then they prefer to fight only those their own age and sex.

The consequences of antisocial behavior are related to the complex of traits surrounding food. As noted in the previous chapter, five- to eight-year-olds are frequently beaten for taking food, though in some cases the food may actually have been consumed by another child or an animal. One of the means for avoiding punishment in this circumstance is for the preadolescent to threaten to swear that the ground or an *oru* should kill him if he is lying. Proposing to make an invocation sometimes averts a beating, but incorrigibles will swear their innocence even when caught in the act. Notwithstanding these few exceptions, most boys and girls recognize the potency of the *orumọ*. By attending funerals, they have learned that *orumọ* are responsible for death. Furthermore, several children name the *orumọ* as the reason it is dangerous to steal.

Stealing is held by most children to be very bad and something they would never do. They admit, however, to having taken food in their own houses without permission, as well as to denying the act to their parents afterwards. The distinction they make between the two acts is significant because it adumbrates the difference between acting within their rights and performing antisocial deeds. Parents reinforce this discrimination by explaining the logic behind their reprimands: to eat all the food during the day simply means there will be none left for the evening meal, but to take food from another house is stealing and an *oru* could be invoked.

Although respect, control of aggression, and aversion to antisocial activities are all related to the functioning of the adult community, the more formal aspects of the political structure are but dimly sensed in this age-period. There is a "consciousness of kind" that preadolescents extend to Opuama Clan as against others, and to Ebiama as opposed to other villages in Opuama, mainly phrased as "this is where I prefer to live," and more diffusely expressed in a distrust of strangers. The section in which he lives is most significant to the child. Here he joins with other relatives to wrestle or play "war"—a mock battle conducted with pieces of dried mud and sticks—against those of another section of the village. Since ties of kinship cut across the whole of Ebiama, the participants say there are "no brothers or sisters" during these matches, a statement that well characterizes adult intersection conflicts.

The only designated political role with which children are familiar is that of village head (*amananawei*). Though this position had long been vacant in Ebiama, juveniles are acquainted with the title because *amananawei* is a frequent character in stories, representing the principal authority in a community.

RELIGION

All children attending school claim they want to continue to be Christians when they grow up. At school they are taught to denigrate Ijaw religious beliefs and to avoid ceremonies connected with cult-houses. Yet, they have faith in the efficacy of the *orumọ,* at the very least, to provide sanctions against stealing. Although the children receive little specific instructions at home regarding the *orumọ* or any other spiritual beings, during preadolescence they become more knowledgeable about them than in previous age-periods.

As part of their growing sophistication, children learn to distinguish between particular *orumọ* (that is, those having personal names) and *orumọ* in general. Men are hesitant to invoke or even mention the name of the most powerful *oru* in Ebiama. Women must not, or bear a heavy fine, and girls, therefore, are especially reminded of this restriction. On the other hand, children mention the word "*oru*" in stories and games without fear, as when one of the characters in a tale swears an *oru* or is killed by one. In one popular game—a type of hide-and-seek— an older girl acts as a "hen" and younger children are her "chicks." Whenever she leaves the playing area to "farm," another child, imitating a hawk, takes away one chick after the other. Each time the hen returns, she swears an *oru,* a broom, a canoe, and so on, to kill the thing which has been stealing her chicks, but all of them are finally taken and she runs to search for them. This profane use of *orumọ* is permitted as long as specific deities are not mentioned by name, thereby avoiding an actual invocation.

Boys actively participate in the secular *owu* dances of adults and usually stop playing their own *owu* game, as described for the previous age-period. Those not too bashful to reveal their dancing ability participate in preliminary festivities the evening before an actual *owu* dance takes place. Dancing without masks, but with leg rattles and holding small sticks to represent machetes, the boys practice the typical steps of the masked dancers. The older men play the drums and correct or compliment them.

Children continue to express much more fear of the forest things (*bouyei*) and the dead (*duwoiyou*) than of the *orumọ,* personalized or general. Now that they are old enough to enter the forest without supervision, they become acutely aware of the dangers and therefore try to avoid going alone. At night they also stay away from certain sections of the village where *duwoiyou* have been seen. In contrast with the previous age-period, they have learned that ancestors reside in villages of the dead and not in the forest. Furthermore, though both ancestors and ghosts are called *duwoiyou,* they are differentiated by the belief that ghosts kill the living by beating them with sticks, while a dead relative would not harm one of his descendants in a direct manner. The *bouyei* are described in a variety of ways by children: they are bodiless heads, dwarfs, and man-like beings with tails. Adults speak of them, and children themselves claim to have heard the sounds they make in the forest, but to see any of them may mean death.

Sorcerers (*diriguọyou*) do not frighten a preadolescent, even though he realizes they are dangerous. As a form of protection, he has come to know that a drink should be tasted by the person serving it to prove it has not been poisoned. His knowledge of *diriguọyou* derives from listening to conservations between grown-ups, and perhaps from observing the swift disposal of the corpse should the deceased be shown to have been a sorcerer. Parents stress the necessity of avoiding contacts with strangers and of being careful not to provoke a sorcerer. A man slapped his ten-year-old son on one occasion for continuing to wear a metal ring, which the father thought might be interpreted by a sorcerer as a mode of protection, requiring a test of his power. Not one child in this age-period queried on the subject of past illnesses thought they were caused by sorcerers.

The only other aspect of cosmology with which juveniles demonstrate an acquaintance is Wọnyinghi and particularly the agreement with Wọnyinghi made by every individual before birth. Wọnyinghi is recognized in a general way as the Creator, the determinant of personal fortune, and to some extent, of personality.

This is apparent in the many stories that include mention of Wọnyinghi and in the reasons several children give for why another child acts strangely or does not want to play with others: "It is his agreement with Wọnyinghi."

We have seen that along with an appreciation of the fatalism engendered by a belief in Wọnyinghi, children in this age-period assume the responsibility, with all its prerequisites of performance in household tasks, of taking care of themselves and younger children. This combination of achievement and world view is a major marker on the road to becoming a fully developed Ijaw.

7/Adolescence from fourteen to seventeen: consolidation for adulthood

THE BEGINNING OF THE FINAL PERIOD of growth and development of the Ijaw child is characterized by the onset of puberty. A girl's pubescence permits her to marry and bear children. Puberty is one indication of a boy's ability finally to undertake several of the more strenuous tasks that men perform. The description of these four years is abbreviated because in many ways adolescent behavior reiterates the ethnography of the adult society at large as presented in Chapter 2.

This period is transitional in somewhat similar fashion as the five- to eight-year-old span. At that time, we saw the child pass from "innocence" and complete dependence on others to a position of responsibility with a partial knowledge of rationalizations for Ijaw behavior. A less dramatic transition occurs as a youth gradually leaves childhood behind to assume the whole cloak of adult life. Two important achievements stand out during adolescence. First, cultural meanings are extensively integrated with behavior in a process that will continue for the rest of an individual's life, and second, the roles of male and female in the division of labor become more sharply defined.

The community does not regard the termination of adolescence as coincident with the arrival of adulthood. Like all divisions of the Ijaw life cycle, adulthood is based on performance, not on attaining a specific age or participating in a *rite de passage*. Marriage, children and, in the case of a man, the ability to provide a house for his family, confer duties of full membership in the adult community. By the age of seventeen most girls have fulfilled the requirements, while young men achieve a full voice in communal and family affairs at about the age of twenty-five or thirty when they first marry.

To return to the analogy suggested earlier, the developed photograph representing a nine- to thirteen-year-old, as he mirrors more of the dimensions of Ijaw culture, now is touched up, with new features appearing in the picture of the males. Furthermore, the misprints in the previous age-period, the incorrigibles who reflect the opposite of what their parents value, disappear. Adolescents exercise their individuality without falling outside the boundaries of permissible variation.

83

ECONOMIC ACTIVITIES

Since nine- to thirteen-year-olds take care of younger children, this task is infrequently imposed on adolescents. Both boys and girls continue to assist in cooking, sweeping, and washing. Their performance reaches adult standards, and it is not unusual to hear a mother report that a daughter, or even a son, of this age can cook as well as herself.

Concerning the economic pursuits girls perform outside the house, most unmarried young women now have their own farms, which they can handle entirely by themselves, leaving their play-farms behind the village to younger siblings. In addition to refining their farming skills, the girls become acquainted with the farming seasons to the point of reminding their mothers when it is time to begin a step in the farming cycle. Of equal importance to her future, a girl at this time learns the location of farms belonging to her parents and relatives, which she will later claim as her own. Schoolgirls do not quite reach the level of competence just described because they are not free to participate in time-consuming undertakings, such as lengthy fishing trips or preparing a farm by themselves. Nonetheless, after school and during school holidays, they are expected to learn the tasks performed by women.

Unlike the continuity in the female division of labor from the last age-period to this one, boys only now begin to make significant strides toward acquiring the skills of men. The best example of their progress is the first time they climb a palm-oil tree and cut down a bunch of nuts. Even though the preparation of palm oil is no longer a common pursuit in Ebiama, adults maintain that youths should become acquainted with it before turning to the more lucrative trade of distilling gin.

There is no specific age at which boys are expected to climb palm trees, and a few, because of illness or their small physical stature, do not begin until they are beyond adolescence. Whatever his age, on obtaining the first bunch of palm nuts a boy brings it to an adult, usually a woman, to perform the *tęnębǫmǫ* (thigh rubbing) for him. She cooks the palm fruit and calls young children and other adolescents in the neighborhood. The children gather handfuls of food and palm nuts while the woman rubs palm oil on the boy's legs. She tells him not to be afraid to climb again, to have fortune finding good bunches of palm fruits, and to avoid snakes at the tops of the trees. As soon as she finishes, the children throw their food at the youth as he dashes for the river, where he will be safe from them. The neophyte palm-cutter should present the next seven bunches of palm fruits he collects to the woman and she in return gives him a small gift.

The *tęnębǫmǫ* described here was performed in every detail by only a few boys of this age-period. Usually, either the first bunch was inadequate and the second one cut was brought, or no additional fruits were given to the person performing the ceremony, or the adult did not reciprocate with a gift. Several boys did not have the ceremony at all, according to one skeptic, because "Those not performing the *tęnębǫmǫ* are still cutting palm, so I did not do it." The young adults whom these boys are imitating claim they did not have the *tęnębǫmǫ* because they believed it would not make them any more or less frightened. The principal disbelievers are Christians with school experience, but the ceremony is not associated with non-Christian worship.

No one can say why the *tẹnẹbọmọ* should make an individual less afraid of climbing palm trees. Men and boys who underwent the ritual remember feeling proud at its conclusion, as friends their own age and adults congratulated them. Probably the expectation of public approval provides a boy with an inducement to overcome his initial fear and ascend at least the first tree.

Once a boy obtains his own bunches of palm nuts, he can continue with the entire manufacturing process of producing palm oil. He carries the fruit to the village, boils the nuts, mashes them in a small trough, sometimes helped by a friend, and sells the oil by the bottle to women in the village.

Achievements in other occupations are not ritually celebrated. A boy learns how to prepare a palm-wine tree for tapping, but he must assist his father or older brother for a long time since distillation equipment is too expensive for him to obtain for himself. Youths participate in the gin trade, helping both to paddle canoes to the Calabar area and to sell the illicit product. They become more proficient at men's fishing techniques: weaving and throwing nets, setting spring traps, and spearing fish at the waterside. A few adolescents attempt to trap small animals, or strive to carve a canoe, but these are precursory endeavors and we find only a small number of talented adults actually employed in hunting or canoe manufacturing.

All this is not to say that an adolescent stops playing games or building the same bird traps as when he was younger. With the attainment of physical maturity, however, he helps his father or other men requesting his aid, or performs those tasks peculiar to adults in the same way that girls, according to Ijaw belief, "naturally" start weaving at the age of five or six. He is informally assisted in learning new tasks by a grown person or a youth already accomplished in them. Once a boy has been taught a task, for example how to cut away the palm leaves to expose the palm fruit, or how to attach a bamboo ladder to a palm-wine tree for the tapping, he is expected to carry on by himself. Moreover, rather than being primarily motivated by a desire to avoid the punishments that so frequently accompanied his learning of previous habits, his motivation is now based upon internalized values or wants.

The basic value manifest here is that work is good in itself, a tenet he has slowly, almost imperceptibly acquired from the time he first learned to perform tasks. Material goals are also important. He desires the food and clothing his parents are less able or willing to provide as their family grows larger. At the same time he himself wants to gain proficiency. He expresses shame when his endeavors are unfavorably compared with his peers, unless he is lazy, which the Ijaw hold to be unnatural.

Parents express satisfaction at their sons' abilities and recognize that the boys will soon be in a position of independence comparable to their own. They therefore refuse to offer an opinion or advice on which adult occupation their child should pursue. As one mother said, "When a boy becomes a man, you cannot tell him what to do. He will do whatever he wants." Nevertheless, most men contradict their own attitude that culture change proceeds too quickly, by hoping their sons, if attending school, will go on to be a teacher or clerical worker, or follow some other calling that will make their schooling useful.

Most of the boys in this age-period are attending school, and almost all of them desire to be teachers or soldiers in the Nigerian army. If these choices were not open, most of them claim they would tap palm wine rather than collect palm fruit because of the additional money and degree of independence the former gives. Those preferring the latter point to the dry working locations and to the possibility of collecting palm bunches at any time during the day, in contrast to the unhealthiness of tapping in the swamps and to the rigid schedule of having to make twice daily collections of the wine.

MARRIAGE

By the age of sixteen or seventeen every girl in Ebiama is married, and most are mothers as well. Betrothal takes place a few years before marriage, but a man should not sleep with his intended spouse or take her to his house to live before her menarche. Since a young woman requires little more knowledge of economic tasks for setting up a household than she has already obtained during her pre-adolescence, we will be primarily concerned here with other attributes of becoming a wife and mother.

In the course of a typical courtship, a young man approaches a girl with the proposal of marriage by giving her small gifts and, if she consents to marry, an "agreement fee" of £1/10. Parents complain that they are the last persons to know their daughter's intention and usually hear about it from a third party who has heard the rumor from still someone else. They may, indeed, remain ignorant until the young man sends messengers to announce that he will come on a specified day to pay the bridewealth. Adolescents, however, infrequently make a point of keeping their future marital plans secret from their parents. Girls often discuss suitors with their mothers and ask for advice, but parents like to underline their impotent position. They insist that they cannot advise a daughter on whom she should marry. By this declaration they unhappily admit to their inability to prevent an undesirable marriage. The attitude of adults in this matter parallels their refusal to advise their sons on what occupation they should undertake. Since a child will make his choice irrespective of their wishes, it is better, most parents believe, not to express any preference. At times, however, they feel constrained to oppose a match and their ineffectualness becomes real. Parents emphatically advise their daughter or son against marriage with a too closely related kinsman. The girl's father might even threaten to refuse the bridewealth, but he would eventually relent, accept the situation, and in a special ceremony ask the ancestors to do likewise.

A girl is neither surprised nor frightened by her menarche. Her mother shows her how to prepare and use moss to absorb menstrual blood. As a preadolescent she observed that women undergo restrictions during their menstrual periods, but her mother makes certain that she is familiar with the taboos. Besides the general prohibition of avoiding all physical contact with males, during menstruation a woman must not pass in front of a certain cult-house, allow fire to be taken from her hearth for use in a cult-house, or cook for a man.

No announcement or ceremony marks the onset of menstruation, but a girl reveals that she has reached physical maturity by observing the necessary restrictions. If she is already promised in marriage, she and her betrothed can secretly begin to have sexual intercourse until he is prepared to pay the bridewealth and officially take her to his house. As noted in previous chapters, children at an early age are familiar with sexual intercourse and Ijaw believe that this is one aspect of the marital relationship that requires no instruction. A girl is told by her mother or friends that she should not step over her husband's legs or assume the top position in sexual intercourse, because these acts are forbidden by the village ancestors (*opu duwoiyou*). Furthermore, she is informed that she should never wash her clothes in the same basin with the clothes of a man.

Even after receiving gifts and money and having intercourse with her intended spouse, it is still possible for a girl to change her mind and accept an offer of marriage from another man. She has only to return the agreement fee. On the other hand, if the girl is promiscuous after promising to marry, and particularly if she is impregnated by another man, her intended husband may retract his offer and demand return of the fee as well as all of his other gifts. This circumstance rarely occurs, since most girls are fearful of acquiring a bad reputation.

Prior to moving to the house of her husband, a girl receives suggestions from her parents on how to establish good relationships with her affines. She is advised to obey her husband (*yei*), as long as he treats her well. A mother-in-law (*yei nyinghi*) and father-in-law (*yei dau*) should receive the same respect due her own parents. Her mother may also suggest that she weave a large number of mats in anticipation of having to reciprocate for the gifts her husband's relatives will give her.

These three affinal relationships, *yei, yei nyinghi,* and *yei dau,* must be newly learned. If one of her brothers is married, an adolescent bride may already know how to behave toward her husband's classificatory brothers and sisters since these affinal terms and the obligations associated with them are reciprocal. Her brother's wife is her *doghǫ* and after she herself marries her husband's siblings are *doghǫ* to her. The *doghǫ* is a joking relationship between a woman and her husband's younger brother in which they may insult and degrade the person or possessions of each other. Since the levirate is practiced, they also are potential mates.

The joking relationship between *doghǫ* is comparable to that of age-mates (*zi ogbo*), and both are more restrained than the freedom allowed in the relationship between sister's husband and wife's siblings (*ǫgǫ*). The kinship term, *ǫgǫ*, like *doghǫ*, is reciprocal. A new bride is, of course, not directly involved in an *ǫgǫ* relationship, which is initiated between her husband and her siblings, though she herself may be an *ǫgǫ* if one of her sisters has married. In addition to the privileges permitted *doghǫ*, two *ǫgǫ* may use stronger insults and call one another sorcerers as long as the accusation is not seriously made. Because the sororate and sororal polygyny are forbidden, those in an *ǫgǫ* relationship are never potential mates.

Although the Ijaw can verbalize the behavior expected from specific kinsmen and affines, the harmony of a relationship largely depends on the individuals involved. The Ijaw believe the personalities of a couple are an important consideration for marital stability. Of course, the nature of this relationship is also influenced by the swiftness with which the woman becomes pregnant, as previously mentioned, and by whether the bride is the first wife. If she is entering a polygynous household, she must adjust to co-wives as well. A man should treat all his wives in equal manner, but since the phenomenon of a man having a "favorite" wife is not uncommon, the potential for conflict is increased by her entry. An ideal is also stated on the relationship between the bride and her mother-in-law. They should respect and help each other. A woman should offer to assist her mother-in-law in farming. Her offer, however, may be refused, perhaps because in this way she would become familiar with the location of farms her husband might then claim for her.

Although good farms are scarce, a woman never acknowledges that a reason for marrying within her own community is to retain farmland belonging to her own consanguineous relatives and thereby avoid being made dependent upon her husband's relatives for land.[1] A woman marrying in her home village behaves as before, maintaining much the same contacts with friends and family, listening to criticisms, and trying to avoid being an object of gossip. A bride from another village enjoys a brief period of cordial non-interference, because she is a stranger, before she too is submitted to the unrelenting critical comments of those living near her. These criticisms are forthcoming to a greater extent after a woman has her first child. Though the new mother usually has considerable experience in caring for infants, older women correct her every time they notice she does something slightly different from patterns typically Ijaw, and specifically those of Ebiama. "People do not do it that way," she is told, and the proper method is described. The rebuke implies that the correction is beyond argument and that the young mother should behave like an adult.

In certain areas of life, adolescents are permitted to make their own decisions and choices. As we have seen, the Ijaw believe a girl can marry whom she wishes, but after marriage she cannot choose among alternative modes of conduct with her family and in her work. In practice, variation occurs because of ignorance of what *the* pattern should be or because of stubbornness, but these are usually momentary affronts to the consensus of opinion. Young married women, for example, who say they would threaten their children with the dead (*duwoiyou*) to stop them from crying are unaware that the *duwoiyou* should not be mentioned for this purpose. On being reprimanded by older women, the younger ones immediately recant and promise never to repeat their mistake.

Since boys are a few years behind girls in learning new occupations, it follows that more time is required for them to acquire the adult roles of husband and father. During adolescence, boys become familiar with relatives in the position of *dǫghǫ* and *ǫgǫ*, but they cannot practice *ǫgǫ* behavior readily since their sisters' husbands would be considerably older than themselves and the respect for age supersedes the privilege of insulting an *ǫgǫ*. In almost all instances, young men must wait until their middle twenties to marry, primarily because they lack the marriage payments. Their attitude toward the opposite sex is perhaps best expressed in their response to what they would do if insulted by a girl their own age. Whereas younger boys do not differentiate between sexes in their responses, adolescents frequently reply that in the case of a female antagonist they would touch her breasts

---

[1] In 1958 only 57 percent of the married women in Ebiama had been born there.

instead of returning her insult. Pubescent boys still occasionally go about without clothes, but for the most part they are not seen naked except during their baths.

The heterosexual play-groups, which were important for the younger children, now completely dissolve, being replaced by sets of a few good friends of the same sex. The basis of friendship rests essentially on compatibility, and the same willingness as when younger to invite a friend to share food, to aid him in times of need, and to avoid quarrels with him. Reciprocity in each criterion is recognized but, compared to the previous age-period, a refinement in practice occurs during adolescence that indicates growing sophistication. One boy astutely observed, "Giving should not be equal among friends, because one person would seem to be 'paying back' what the other had done for him." The amount given in return by a comrade, whether it be food or a gift, should be slightly less or more than the amount received.

SOCIAL CONTROL

There are no incorrigibles among the adolescents of Ebiama. This could be a matter of chance. Conceivably, the children we observed during our stay in Ebiama are not a typical cross-section of Ijaw childhood. The fourteen- to seventeen-year-olds may have been well-behaved as preadolescents, and the incorrigibles mentioned in Chapter 6 may not change on becoming adolescents. It appears more likely that the responsibilities of approaching adulthood and maturing sensitivity, expressed in ideas such as that of unequal reciprocity, modify most antisocial behavior. A teenage person, who fails to learn tasks that will make him independent of his parents, would find it difficult to marry or even to survive. Thus he has little alternative but to conform, in major outline, to what is expected of him. Social control also becomes more effective in this age-period because adolescents profess to respect age difference and the superior knowledge of older persons.

Adolescents refer to the *orumọ* as the reason why one should not take anything that belongs to someone else. They also know the rules of invoking an *oru* to support their claim of innocence if falsely accused. The consequences of an invocation are now fully understood and an adolescent will not threaten to swear an *oru* without good reason. Although the *orumọ* are believed to be one of the prime mechanisms for the control of antisocial behavior, and government force and restraint are British innovations, older children fear and often mention the police and the prison in tales. Even though neither is found in Ebiama itself, police occasionally visit in the area to implement a court order or to arrest an offender.

RELIGION

Adolescents understand and appreciate the power of the *orumọ,* but they have little direct contact with them. The *orumọ* are served by parents or older siblings, and those in this age-period are still not allowed to enter the one secret cult-house in Ebiama.

Youths are as skeptical about diviners (*buroyou*) as adults. In stories and in response to hypothetical questions, the *burokęmę* is the character capable of treachery. He maliciously gives "bad medicine" instead of curative herbs and "says anything" when asked to divine the cause of some misfortune or what the future offers, just to receive his fee. Even though doubt is constantly cast on the prescient ability of the diviner, incredulity is rarely directed toward the belief system itself. Adolescents, like adults, perceive the realities of death, accident, and ill luck, and they accept the existence of a causal connection between misfortunes and *orumǫ* or *diriguoyou*. Because a *burokęmę* is human, divination is liable to human error, particularly since diviners depend on their own visions as well as on a variety of paraphernalia. Nonetheless, skepticism of diviners in general is by no means a rejection of all of them. Many adolescents are convinced the *buroyou* living in Ebiama have power, while most of the others believe that diviners living elsewhere could provide them with magical medicines for becoming a good wrestler, student, or lover.

The use of the *obębę* (ladder) in divining is another illustration of a matter about which both adolescents and adults are skeptical. Many persons express doubt that the *obębę* used during funerals is moved by the *tęmę* of the deceased. They believe the four men carrying it are the true movers. On the other hand, those doubting the efficacy of a funeral *obębę* have subsequently carried a special *obębę* for wrestlers, belonging to a particular forest *oru,* and avow that something actually moves them. Even though these young men agree that an outside force is responsible for the movement itself, they still doubt the answers given by the *obębę.* On one occasion the *obębę* proved wrong in predicting that Ebiama would win an important wrestling match, and doubters were quick to point out its mendacity.

In less important areas of behavior, adolescents begin to question what they formerly accepted as true. A child, who would earlier attribute strange noises in the night to the "dead" or "forest people," now considers the possibility that they are made by a goat or a wild animal.

The age span from fourteen to seventeen is the most difficult to characterize by any succinct phrase because, aside from a girl assuming additional kinship obligations through her marriage and a boy becoming adept at adult occupations, very little that is learned can be described as entirely new in their enculturative experience. What has been acquired previously is now practiced and consolidated as virtually the final step to adult status. If any individuals were unable to adjust socially in the previous age-period, by now they have been socialized, and what we find are individual variations in capacity for leadership and in the skepticism expressed toward aspects of beliefs in nonhuman powers. This variation in itself reflects adult responses, and the expression of doubt must be thought of as a part of the enculturation of young men and women in the same way as learning to paddle a canoe was for children. Yet those questioning the tenets of their culture are few. At most they attempt to integrate their experiences and knowledge within acceptable boundaries of behavior. For most residents of Ebiama the knowledge they acquire of their culture and society gradually expands with few significant changes from the base solidified during adolescence.

8 / Cultural and social change

ULTURAL AND SOCIAL CHANGE in two different dimensions of Ijaw life were presented in previous chapters. First, Ebiama was set forth as it appeared in 1958–1959, incorporating both traditional traits and recent innovations in the description of the adult community. Then, a developmental set of changes was considered by tracing variations in behavioral and ideational traits acquired by children from one age-period to the next. By interrelating these two dimensions we may explore the extent to which stability in the first can be said to have been affected by the chronology of the second. Why have certain traits in the adult culture remained comparatively stable while others have not? Can this differential be explained by reference to the learning experiences of childhood? In brief, the objective of our investigation is to examine one of the processes underlying differential rates of change.

Since our description of Ebiama is synchronic, we must infer change rather than measure it over a period of time. Yet, this community appears to be an opportune place for pursuing the questions posed above because influence from the external British and Nigerian societies has stimulated change in some areas of belief and behavior but not in others. Furthermore, the changes are gradual, generally affecting only a portion of the population at a time. The new traits of behavior and belief can be delineated by observing the variations that exist within the community, and by asking village elders, who personally witnessed the introduction of the innovations, to distinguish old customs from new ones. The establishment of British dominion in the Niger Delta at the turn of the century clearly falls within this period.

Elements of Ijaw belief and behavior either rejected by the entire population of Ebiama or accepted to a like degree fall outside the scope of our analysis. These changes are of three types. First, there are customs reported to have been traditional, but no longer practiced. These include: men using bull-roarers to frighten children and pregnant women, pregnant women avoiding a certain part of the forest, killing children whose upper teeth appear first, and parents tasting feces should their children do so. Clitoridectomy, similarly, is thought to have once been performed on all females, but is now abhorred by the people of Opuama Clan. Whether these actions occurred or have in some way been introduced as part of a mythological past cannot be ascertained, but the logic of the activities requires that they be practiced in late adolescence or adulthood. Their loss would, therefore, be in accordance with the early learning hypothesis. The second and third types of change confirm the hypothesis for the same reason. The second includes traits that have been added to Ijaw life: recording of gifts to children and at funerals, using English names and adding father's name to one's own, believing in vampires, and replacing what were undoubtedly the predominant male occupations of hunting and fishing during the pre-European contact period with palm oil production and gin distilling. The last category includes shifts in timing or in emphasis, rather than trait losses or additions. Examples here are: male circumcision at infancy, the amount paid a midwife, and men feeling free to punish their sons without the consent of their wives' brothers.

To gauge the pertinence of the early learning hypothesis, we must examine differential changes in adult society and culture and in the existing educational profile. Thus far the school has not drastically affected this profile, but as a further precaution in our analysis its influence must be assessed before turning to the various changes in adult life.

SCHOOLING

The school buildings, made of concrete blocks with corrugated iron roofing, are located at the south end of the village. There is a total of 213 boys and 43 girls enrolled in eight grades, consisting of introductory Classes I and II, followed by Standards I to VI. Each is held in a separate classroom. Standards V and VI met for the first time in 1956 and 1957, respectively. A large percentage of the pupils in these two Standards come from surrounding villages that do not have advanced classes. The visiting students reside with friends or relatives in Ebiama during the school sessions. Prior to 1956, Ebiama children also had to travel to distant villages to complete their primary education. Each class was added in Ebiama as proper facilities were built. Standards III and IV were introduced in the early 1950s and Standards I and II in the 1940s. The first teacher, a Nembe Ijaw, came to the village about 1915 to conduct Christian services and to teach English, but it was not until the early 1920s that the Niger Delta Pastorate took formal charge of schooling as part of its proselytizing program.

One reason schooling has thus far been a minor factor in the acculturation of the community is the short amount of time individuals have been exposed to foreign education. Of more significance than the time element, however, are the proportionally larger attendance by boys than girls and the content of the schooling process itself.

There are no girls enrolled in Standards III or VI, one in Standard V, and two in Standard IV. Only two women in the community had attended school long enough to be able to speak English. Although children from the age of nine must fulfill important duties in the household, boys are usually relieved of these responsibilities on school days. Parents see schooling as a basis for fruitful employment for their sons, but the same is not considered to be true for daughters. Girls will marry and take up the traditional occupations—raising children, caring for the house, and farming and fishing. Therefore, parents, or parental surrogates, hesitate to "invest," by paying fees, in the schooling of girls. The past experience of girls who have continued with their primary education only to be made pregnant by schoolboys or teachers before finishing, also dissuades parents from encouraging their daughters to attend and discourages adolescent girls themselves from going to school. Since few girls complete their primary education and since women and their older daughters act as the principal enculturative agents for the young children, schooling has had minimal repercussion on the education of the young in the home.

The impact of education in the school has also been minimized by inadequately trained teachers. All the instructors in Ebiama are Ijaw, some of whom are natives of the village. After completing a year or two of teacher training at one of the training centers in the Niger Delta they return home or to other Ijaw villages to teach. With so few years of schooling themselves, and with their early enculturation greatly influenced by the nonschool agents previously mentioned, it is little wonder that the teachers confuse many of the foreign ideas transmitted in the schools. Taboo, for example, is defined for the children as tatoo. Explanations for behavior are also reinterpreted. The Headmaster says, for example, it is foolhardy for Standard VI boys to try to pass their final examinations, administered by the Regional Government, by drawing "magical signs" on their papers to distract the graders. He advises the students against these machinations because he believes the graders pass their own magical charms over the stack of examinations, causing any papers magically treated to "fly out" onto the floor and to be graded as failures.

Attendance in a school might be regarded as one of the crucial variables in the acculturation of several adults in Ebiama. These exceptions, however, had additional influential experiences. First, since they had to complete their primary schooling in other Delta villages or on the mainland, their residence away from Ebiama may have been as effective in acculturating them as the coincident occurrence of their formal education. Second, a selective factor may have been operative by which parents permitted bright and ambitious children likely to succeed to continue their education because the school fees seemed a worthwhile investment. Thus, besides schooling, experience and innate ability must be weighed as shaping individual responses during acculturation.

The importance of the school presumably will increase rapidly due to the addition of higher Standards and the financial encouragement given to both boys and girls to attend. In 1957 the Government announced that school fees would be abolished the following year, but this order was revised in 1958 to a gradual reduction in fees. Classes I and II and Standard I were free as of that year, and fees were to be eliminated one class at a time in each successive year.

From its beginnings the school has been intimately related to Christianity. Religion is taught during school hours, students are required to attend church services, which are held in the classrooms every day, morning and evening, and one of the school teachers acts as the lay preacher for the community services on Sunday. One of the main objectives of the teachers is to persuade the children to refuse to serve the *orumọ*, and a pupil found participating in any way in a "pagan" ceremony is severely criticized. Children (even many of those who do not attend school) profess to be Christians, but conversion has proved tenuous for many individuals after they reach adulthood. The affirmations of the children, therefore, cannot be taken as a conclusive change away from the *orumọ*. Furthermore, the complex of traits involving the *orumọ* comprise more than actual participation in ceremonies.

There are a number of other potential changes associated with schooling, which though more subtle than those having to do with religion, may become equally influential. The traditional pattern of authority predicates that age demands deference, but authority rests with those who possess the qualities to foster agreement among the majority. The pattern of authority between teacher and student is quite different, since here deference and obedience are paid to an office rather than to an individual, and the power of that office is paramount. Although parents occupy a somewhat analogous position to teachers, parental authority tends to be diffused among other adult relatives once a child is old enough to run to them for protection.

The school system, ignoring the traditional qualifications for command, places children in a situation from which there is no escape, in the sense that parents usually not only support the teacher, but often go a step further in requesting that the Headmaster mete out disciplinary measures for offenses their children commit at home. It is impossible in this case to separate cause from effect. Did parents first call upon teachers to punish their children, thereby shifting more authority to the instructors, or did the school staff, impressing both parents and students alike with their superior knowledge of European traditions, first assume these powers? In any event, the prestige accorded the position of the school teacher has started to change traditional authority patterns; and one unfortunate consequence of schooling, according to the unanimous opinion of adults, is the display of disobedience by children toward their parents and elders. As the teacher becomes more important there could be a corresponding effect on the transmission of traditional customs as the children try to imitate the image of modernity projected by him.

The understanding children acquire of a particular office as being superordinate, by extension, portends a significant initial step in the appreciation of the Regional and Federal Governments of Nigeria as political hierarchies. In contrast to the stateless type of Ijaw political organization based on kinship, a national government requires its members to accept authority vested in specific offices, ranging from policeman to prime minister, that must be obeyed regardless of the individual —Ijaw or not—filling a given role. More explicitly, schooling prepares the children for participation in the national regime by instructing them in the history and geography of Africa, and by informing them about their identity as Nigerians as well as Ijaw. Students do not automatically become patriotic by recognizing national boundaries, but even knowing about the world outside their own village and the Niger Delta adumbrates an incipient nationalism and provides a striking contrast with the elders of the community to whom the concept and word "Nigeria" are untranslatable in Ijaw.

There are still other ways schooling could have lasting effects on the community. On completion of a Standard VI education, a student tends to disparage the thought of turning to the traditional Ijaw manual occupations, but wishes instead to obtain a lucrative post that will permit him both to utilize the literacy skills he has acquired and to earn money. In the past, teaching provided the main outlet for those few who completed their primary schooling. Now, with almost all the boys attending the upper primary classes, there will be an insufficient number of positions for them, and the political and economic repercussions could be extensive. As Lewis points out for Nigeria as a whole, "There is no political situation more likely to cause difficulties for the Government than one in which the economy of the country is not capable of absorbing the products of the [educational] system at the various points at which they leave it" (1965:143).

Two conclusions can be drawn from the preceding statements concerning the role of schooling and its proper relation to cultural and social change in Ebiama. First, several factors—that boys, in the vast majority, rather than girls attend school; that until the introduction of upper classes to Ebiama in 1956 only a few children were able to conclude their primary education; and finally, that the foreign stimulus intended in the curriculum has been reinterpreted by the inadequately trained teaching staff—have all contributed to minimizing the acculturative effect of the school and to inhibiting children from acting as enculturative agents in the society at large. Second, despite its insignificance for most people in the past, the school promises to be of great importance in the future, particularly for religious beliefs, political awareness, and economic occupations, as more and more children of both sexes complete their primary education.

THREE AREAS OF CHANGE

Economic, political, and religious systems represent conventional aspects of Ijaw culture and society in which the external pressure for change, despite considerable differences, is most in evidence. The least direct pressure has been applied to the economic system. Taxes must be paid, but the means for acquiring the necessary funds have been left open. The greatest direct influence brought to bear on the community is the government (the British Government and then the independent Eastern Regional Government of Nigeria) in the form of district officers, and laws and directives backed by a police force. Religion offers a middle ground between the first two aspects. Because of the mission school an effort has been aimed at changing the traditional religious system, but force is absent. The cultural and social changes within each of these major aspects will be taken up in turn, incorporating the overt reasons for change and the relation of early or late learning to the innovations.

Economic Organization   The least direct acculturative pressure has been applied in the realm of economic organization, but one of the most obvious changes has been taking place here. Starting in the 1930s, and increasingly since World War II, the men have shifted their occupations from the manufacture of palm oil to distilling gin. Concomitantly, the production unit of a man and his wife or wives has replaced the cooperative work force consisting of the adult men of the community.

Ebiama men explain this change in occupations by their desire for economic independence and for a higher income, and by the opportunity to avoid the obligation to cooperate in mashing palm fruit. A distiller enjoys a "seller's market," since gin is always in demand and there are usually more buyers than sellers. This condition contrasts with the position of a man who produces palm oil and kernels and must depend entirely on one buyer, the United Africa Company, whose agents, reportedly, sometimes take advantage of their monopoly and refuse to buy the produce unless personally compensated. Furthermore, most men claim distilling gin provides a higher annual income than making palm oil.

On the other hand, men complain about the leeches in the swamps where the palm wine trees grow, and the illnesses they contract there. They also stress how hard it is to tap the palm trees twice daily, as must be done if the sap is not to spoil or the tree die prematurely. The main advantages of collecting palm fruits are the healthy working conditions and the small effort required to produce the palm oil. Nevertheless, with the great value Ijaw place on work, the difficulties of tapping are not considered sufficient to balance the advantages derived from distilling gin.

At the same time the men have been changing their occupations, the women have retained their traditional tasks, explicitly rejecting, for the most part, the relatively new opportunities to trade that have presented themselves. A few men say that they would not discourage their wives from trading, and claim they would even go so far as to advance capital for a trading venture. Most husbands, however, are unenthusiastic at the prospect of women trading because they suspect a woman who trades will supplement her income by prostitution, or will make sufficient money to repay her bridewealth and divorce whenever she chooses. Many women also frown on this occupation because they do not consider it "work"—manual labor—even though trading proves to be more profitable than fishing or farming for those few attempting it.

The behavior involved in the division of labor supports the early learning hypothesis. Between the ages of five and eight, girls already mirror the tasks of women, and between nine and thirteen become proficient at their work. Boys, on the other hand, only begin to attempt the work of men as they reach the age of responsibility, and hardly attain proficiency in many tasks until their twenties. Those occupations associated with the male side of the division of labor are seen to have changed much more readily than those performed by the women.

The shift in male occupational patterns has necessitated only minor technological changes, since the metal drums and piping required for distilling gin are purchased from the United Africa Company or from traders in the same way as the iron machetes, axes, and kettles used in preparing palm oil must be obtained. Profits from both occupations are also used in the same way. The villagers purchase consumer items as quickly as they accumulate the money to do so. They seem unwilling to keep on hand any excess cash that might be quickly dissipated by relatives or used up to meet the demands of unforeseen difficulties. Manufactured and purchased items act as investments which, unlike money, may be retained by the owner. "Hard goods" are important determinants of status as well.

With the emphasis on obtaining items of prestige, the introduction of newly valued goods represents more a reinterpretation of traditional pattern than any significant adjustment of the traditional economic system itself. Roofing made of corrugated iron sheets is a substitute for big-dowry wives, who are becoming too expensive and dangerous to obtain since the Government interprets their acquisition as illegal slavery. Only one dwelling in Ebiama has a corrugated iron roof, but several men are patiently accumulating bundles of the roofing material and plan to erect houses within a few years.[1] The readiness to accept new material items supports the early learning hypothesis in that those articles mentioned are only of interest to adolescent and adult Ijaw. Whether adults would be willing to give up the machete and its manner of use in farming and cutting grass—bending from the waist and slashing with a wrist action—would be revealing in this context, since toy machetes are given to children at an early age.

The ideational aspects of these changes have been slight since the basic values in the division of labor remain stable. Women produce food for household consumption while men participate in the cash economy, enabling them to purchase manufactured items and imported foodstuff. Ijaw disapproval of the occupation of trader for women can be seen as an attempt to maintain values associated with traditional activities, values learned by children as early as the five- to eight-year-old period before girls are old enough to participate in trading ventures. The early emphasis on manual labor, used as part of the rationale for keeping women from trading, appears in the parental desire to keep children busy at routine tasks about the house. Evidence that the boys and girls internalize this value is found in their verbal recognition that a good child is one who obeys the wishes of his parents. The conception of work gains further significance by being identified with the feeling of responsibility an individual must have for himself and others, a trait learned during the "transitional" age-period and put to full practice by those between nine and thirteen.

Giving up cooperative work-groups, like those needed for producing palm oil, in favor of units limited to the household points not to an abandonment of values laid on cooperation and reciprocity, but rather to an attempt to maintain these very values. The group of men required to mash palm fruits was large and problems of sharing equally in the work often arose. When the alternative of distilling palm wine became available, it was accepted fairly readily (Leis 1964). Smaller cooperative units, based primarily on residential ties, continue to function. The village populace organizes itself into these units to build houses for school teachers or to clear forest paths. The value of cooperation is inculcated in the earliest age-period, as when parents commend infants for sharing their food. Children from five to eight interpret sharing and cooperation to be highly approved modes of action, and good deeds, they believe, should be reciprocated.

A minority of the community, indirectly affected by schooling and for reasons already stated in Chapter 2, have attempted to institute patrilineal inheritance. Despite the unlikelihood of their living longer than their offspring, fathers reason that since they pay for the maintenance and often the school fees for their sons, they, rather than their son's maternal relatives, should inherit any wealth left by their children. In turn, young men who have been to school and learned about the inheritance rules of Europeans believe they should have a claim to the property of their fathers. One of the major factors in this argument is the more permanent

---

[1] In the village only two buildings (the school and a cult-house) have both corrugated iron roofs and concrete floors.

type of concrete block housing being contemplated in Ebiama, and already built in some of the neighboring villages. The question of who should inherit such a house, the son living there or the son of the deceased's sister living in another village, becomes a real issue in contrast to the much less permanent wattle-and-daub house which was never given serious consideration in the past. Although the courts support the traditional line of inheritance in disputes of this sort in other villages, a growing desire for patrilineal inheritance is apparent and a change in this direction found expression in one of the recommendations of the Clan Council.

Except for those cases of a child actually brought up in the home of his mother's brother, or receiving his school fees and additional support from his maternal relatives, the patrilocal kin group is of first importance from the point of view of the young, and it is not until later childhood—between the ages of nine and thirteen—that the wider implications of kinship terms are clearly recognized.

Political Organization   The Ijaw have accepted with resignation the innovations in political structure introduced by the British and enlarged upon by the Regional Government. They have elected village heads, clan chiefs, and representatives to local and district councils. These offices were filled in Ebiama and Opuama only after great debate and under an aura of distrust displayed by a large part of the community. Ostensibly, the difficulties encountered in electing and installing the village head and clan chief can be attributed to the improbability that any large group would, under these conditions of imposed change, easily and unanimously approve of the same leader, and this is borne out by the problem of selection found in many other nearby Ijaw clans. The resistance to electing officials whose duties and rights were uncertain, but who would represent, regulate, and perhaps profit in their new posts also illustrates a structural conflict that results when an acephalous political organization is forced to realign itself in terms of a system characterized by a hierarchy of offices.

For us, the important point is that this innovative pyramiding of political offices has no parallel change in the traditional concepts of authority. The essential authority continues to rest with those who have the ability to persuade and to obtain a majority vote. Four-year-old Ebiama children seem to practice political behavior in their games, as when a child leads others in make-believe even though he might be younger than his playmates. By the five- to eight-year-old age-period, we found that children too aggressive in trying to assume leadership in games were rejected by their peers, so that by the age of nine or ten, groups maintained their identity only so long as mutual consensus could be achieved. In this case, it is evident that both the behavioral trait of exerting leadership and the ideational trait of expressly denying the role of "leader" and emphasizing communal consensus are learned early.

Another illustration of reaction to formal authority relates to a committee of women appointed by the men to make occasional inspections of the community to insure that regional sanitation laws were being observed. Even though all the committee members were respected and prominent, once they attempted to perform their duties, the other women showed resentment and openly insulted them. In consequence, the committee stopped making its rounds. Though it might be argued that some women simply did not want to repair their houses, and that resistance lay here rather than against authority as such, the reaction of the village women was expressly directed toward the committee members. This set of traits supports the hypothesis of early learning since the patterning of authority has remained stable, inhibiting the selection of officers.

The procedure of the Native Court at Rotoma closely resembles that of the indigenous practice of taking disputes to a respected third party for mediation. Unlike the traditional pattern, however, the decisions of the judges are binding and backed by police force. A district officer occasionally visits Rotoma to hear appeals. This type of power is welcomed by those who feel they have legitimate grievances, but cases are brought to the court only as a last resort. Despite governmental disapproval of the practice, settlement of most disputes is first attempted within the village, where both sides lay the issue before a disinterested third party. Dissatisfaction with the Native Court is based on several grounds, as mentioned in Chapter 2. These include the long distance to the court house, the time wasted waiting for the case to be heard, and the increased expenses of litigation. The possibility that the judges can be bribed also weighs heavily against the formal procedure.

The distinction in conflict settlement between innovation and stability pertains to the extended meaning given judicial procedure under Pax Britannica. In the past a case that was not resolved satisfactorily could lead to direct retaliation. The Native Courts are supposed to prevent blood feuds or any other kind of aggressive retaliation by providing a peaceful means for settlement, with the transfer of responsibility for punishing the guilty party to the State. Settling conflicts by peaceful arbitration, however, runs contrary to a pertinent theme of retaliation that is stressed throughout childhood. Since armed feuds, at least, have not occurred in recent times, here is an example of a trait whose behavioral and ideational aspects are acquired as early as the first age-period, but which has been abandoned by adults in the acculturative situation in favor of redress by the courts and police action. If this observation is accurate, it contradicts the hypothesis of early learning since a trait learned early in life has been readily changed. However, reports from communities more acculturated than Ebiama indicate the Ijaw used guns in one village to try to settle a dispute in 1950, and inhabitants of another settlement were on the verge of doing the same in 1959. According to the Ijaw in Ebiama, they themselves would act similarly given the proper circumstances. Certainly the high incidence of fist fights and wrestling at Ebiama suggests that the Ijaw feel brute strength is an appropriate way to settle many arguments, particularly in a critical situation.

The Opuama Clan Council has attempted to provoke change in several traditional modes of behavior that have not fallen directly under the domain of Nigerian law. The "laws" passed by the Clan Council must be first accepted by each of the villages and their enforcement is based wholly upon mutual consent. Two suggestions of the Council, accepted by most of those in Ebiama, are the setting of bridewealth at £12, and the release of widows from the traditional practice of sleeping on the ground for three days after the death of their husbands. Since both of these practices take on significance comparatively late in the life cycle, they are evidence for the contention that traits learned later in life change more readily than those learned before the age of nine.

In another instance, the Council's suggestion was not accepted. If a big-dowry wife commits adultery, she must hold a huge heavy clay pot on her head while propitiations are made to the ancestors of the village. The Council decided the practice should be stopped, but a big-dowry wife in Ebiama is still punished in this way for committing adultery, despite a professed acceptance of the Council's ruling. In one case, a man disliked his big-dowry wife and refused to cohabit with her. Her extramarital affairs, therefore, were for a long time tactfully ignored. The husband became seriously ill, however, and diviners and elders decided that the ancestors had been angered by the failure to propitiate them for the infidelity of his wife. Since this behavioral trait must also be acquired comparatively late in life, its retention is in contradiction to the early learning hypothesis.

Religion   Religious organization and ideology have been more exposed to direct foreign influences than the economic system but less so than the political system. Christianity was peacefully introduced to Ebiama about 1915 simultaneously with the school, and the connection between schooling and religion has already been discussed. The school teacher responsible for the church services is assisted once or twice a year by a pastor or catechist of the Niger Delta Pastorate. Although adults have never been vigorously proselytized, close to 60 percent of the men and 15 percent of the women call themselves Christians. Only ten people are communicants. The definition of a "Christian," as the residents of Ebiama use the term, depends on three criteria. First and foremost, a Christian abstains from participating in any ritual associated with the *orumọ*. Second, he does not employ diviners and looks askance at their activities. Finally, a Christian disavows the killing of twins. The opposite of each of these should characterize the non-Christian, but the differences prove to be ideal expectations and persons claiming affiliation with the church tend to be ambivalent in their beliefs and behavior.

For most adults, the choice between Christianity and the worship of *orumọ* often comes to rest on one major consideration, survival. Illness and death are frequent occurrences in Ebiama and the high death rate of children is particularly grievous. Since an *oru* often demonstrates its wish to be served by bringing sickness to a man or one of his relatives, a Christian finds himself reconsidering his position relative to the *orumọ* whenever he or his children fall ill. Furthermore, the purpose served by an *oru*, to protect and to cure, offers an explanation for the vagaries of daily life, which is not thought by many Ijaw to be adequately fulfilled by the Christian deity. This doubt is illustrated by the failure of a Christian sect, called the Cherubim and Seraphim, to become well established in Ebiama. A large number of converts joined the sect at its introduction in 1946 because cures were promised solely through prayer and the drinking of "blessed water." After these measures failed during a smallpox epidemic in 1948, most of the members returned to the worship of *orumọ*, and the few remaining adherents rarely gather for services.

Contrary to what has just been said, the Ijaw have a perception of faith that could work to support Christian conversion and to vitiate the belief in *orumọ*. Ijaw say they have a strong temptation to join the church because Christians, supposedly, are not subject to the capriciousness of the aboriginal deities who may demand offerings from a propitiant one day and harm him or his children the next. A balance between the possibility and the danger of disbelief appears to be struck in some households by the husband belonging to the church and his wife serving an *oru*.

Cult members maintain there is no essential difference between Christians and themselves because Wǫnyinghi and the Christian God are the same. Indeed, the Ijaw word for "God" in Christian services is "Wǫnyinghi." Those who serve *orumǫ* occasionally attend church services without any feeling of contradiction. Christians, on the other hand, assert that a great gulf exists between the two belief systems, since non-Christians worship "idols," that is, *orumǫ*. Nevertheless, the ability of the *orumǫ* to punish thieves is universally recognized. A Christian may ask a non-Christian to invoke a deity to insure return of what has been stolen. Similarly, as mentioned above, a Christian does not discourage his wife from propitiating an *oru*, especially to combat illness in the family.

Another example of ambivalence is the behavior of Christian women during their menstrual periods. The cult-house for one deity, that forbids menstruating women to cross on the land in front of its dwelling, stands between the school and the main portion of the village. Women during their menses either miss the church services or avoid the cult-house by traveling by canoe to the school building. The punishment for breaking this taboo is continual bleeding until the *oru* is propitiated, an embarrassment the Christian women would rather avoid. So pervasive is this belief that Christians contemplate building a church in a more convenient location. Avoiding certain foods associated with *orumǫ*, as well as certain areas of the forest where *orumǫ* and "forest things" are believed to reside, provide more examples of how Christians have retained traits, behavioral and ideational, that are part of the traditional religious system.

Children participate at about the same time in both *orumǫ* ceremonies and activities associated with diviners. Whereas children from the earliest age observe the public serving of *orumǫ*, they often are participants or recipients of procedures used by diviners to treat illnesses. They also have roles in ceremonies to change "agreements with Wǫnyinghi," and in the rituals for a pregnant woman who has passed the normal time for parturition. These activities are not initially related to ideational traits. Children express some fear of the *orumǫ* only during the period from five to eight, and not until the "age of responsibilty" do they begin to comprehend the power of these beings. Furthermore, an individual cannot propitiate an *oru* himself or visit a diviner of his own accord until a thorough understanding of ideational traits has been achieved and the propitiator can afford the expense.

This sequence of traits is illustrated by the acquisition of esoteric knowledge associated with the cult-house of the most important *oru* in Ebiama. Infant boys, if circumcised, can be brought into the shrine, but once they learn to speak they are excluded until they can be trusted, at the age of eighteen or older, not to report what has occurred within the building. Children, then, participate early in rituals directed at *orumǫ* or conducted by diviners. They learn relevant ideational traits later, in the period from age five until adolescence, and finally, later still, perform the actual behavioral traits of propitiation and consultation.

Adult converts and those brought up as Christians are completely negative toward both the abilities and paraphernalia of the diviners. The Christian view is in part the logical extreme of the general pessimism shown by the non-Christians for their local prophets. More consequently, the instrumental role of the diviners in relating effects to causes usually necessitates the propitiation of *orumǫ*, which by definition, is antithetical to Christian belief and practice.

The data above support the following conclusions. First, behavioral traits involved in personal propitiation of *orumǫ* are practiced considerably later in life than the age at which related ideational traits are learned. The greater persistence of the latter in the conversion of Ijaw to Christianity supports the hypothesis of early learning. The behavioral traits, characterized as avoidance restrictions based on deference for the *orumǫ*, contradict the hypothesis because they appear to be maintained regardless of the age at which they are acquired. Second, the behavioral and ideational aspects of divination are learned at the same time as those involving the *orumǫ,* but the rejection of the diviners as compared with the continuing respect for *orumǫ* contradicts the hypothesis.

The third criterion defining a Christian is his attitude toward twin births. Traditionally, Ijaw consider the birth of twins a calamity. Cult-houses are closed at the birth of twins in the village, and the parents of twins are forbidden to come into contact with the *orumǫ* or their priests until they have a "normal" birth. Christians desire the birth of twins and wish to prove to the non-Christians that no harm will come to the village if the children are allowed to grow up. Adults agree that for as long as they can remember, at least one twin birth a year is not unusual for Ebiama, and two sets of twins were born while we were there. The ubiquitous presence of children allows them, between the ages of five and eight, to become aware of the anxiety that is manifested at the time of these frequent births, but an ideational component is minimal for reasons given below. The age of practicing the twin taboo and the volatility of the trait during acculturation confirms the early learning hypothesis.[2]

The killing of twins and its relationship to enculturation has particular relevance to our analysis. We have here a trait that is the object of vigorous disapproval by the Church and its followers, who threaten to report to the police non-Christians suspected of starving their infants to death. The mission is just as adamant regarding the *orumǫ*, but we have seen that certain attitudes and behavior toward the latter have been retained by the Christians. Why, then, should they be determined to change this particular trait?

One explanation may be the absence of myth that would serve to interpret the killing of twins. No one, not even cult priests, can offer a rationale that explains the association of twins with religious concepts, nor to any specific consequence of allowing twins to survive. This example suggests that the stability of a trait depends on the degree to which it is interrelated with other behavioral and ideational traits. Twin infanticide has the characteristics of a survival that has lost its meaning but is retained by an emotional, inexplicit connection to the *orumǫ*. Conversely,

---

[2] In an earlier statement (Leis 1964), twin infanticide was taken to contradict the hypothesis because children at an early age are exposed to the anxiety created by twin births. Reconsidering the minimal ideational attributes of twins (Leis 1965) led us to the present conclusion.

Christianity offers explicit reasons for giving up the custom, and, given the pervasive Ijaw desire for rearing as many children as possible, the birth of twins comes to be interpreted by Christians as a welcome phenomenon.

The criteria offered to distinguish self-professed Christians from non-Christians (believers in traditional Ijaw religion) comprise the areas of religious belief and practice that have undergone the greatest change. By contrast, both Christians and cult members are similar in adhering to polygynous marriage, which has had some external impetus for change, and to sorcery beliefs.

As with *orumọ* and twin infanticide, the Niger Delta Pastorate opposes polygynous marriage. Men with more than one wife are forbidden to teach in their schools, to marry in church, or to take communion. Allowances are sometimes made for women married to polygynists, since the "sin" is considered to belong to their husbands. Despite the emphasis placed upon monogamous marriage, only one man in Ebiama, a teacher, married his wife in church. It is common knowledge that the other school teachers secretly maintain more than one mate. There is certainly no indication that the church has made any progress among the general populace and Christians and non-Christians alike continue to marry as many women as possible. Polygyny, then, is proving stable even though a stimulus for change, quite strong in the case of the mission teachers, is present.

The process of enculturation as concerns this trait may be broken down into its behavioral and ideational components. Marriage for men does not occur until their twenties, or, for secondary marriage, until their thirties. Growing up in a polygynous household could be taken as a form of passive behavioral participation, but comparable to the way in which children receive food at the propitiation of *oru*, its significance for the socialization of marital behavior seems relatively slight.

The ideational side of polygyny, by contrast, particularly with respect to the most important function of marriage, is learned early. By the age of seven or eight, boys and girls verbalize their desire to have children. This value continues to be held throughout the life of every Ijaw, becoming more emphatic in later years with the recognition that respect and the elaborateness of funeral rites are predicated on the number of progeny. There is one qualification to this observation. A few boys in Standards IV through VI claim they would prefer only one or two wives because additional wives would produce more children than they could afford to keep in school. Similar exceptions are not found among adults. Children, like adults, believe a polygynous household is a more efficient unit than a monogamous one, particularly from the point of view of the male, since wives contribute both foodstuffs and their labor to the maintenance of the home. From the standpoint of females, co-wives share the tasks about the house and the burden of assisting the husband in his work, and if they remain on good terms, provide companionship for one another.

Polygyny both contradicts and supports the hypothesis of early learning. On the one hand, we find polygyny to be stable even though its behavioral aspects are not practiced until later in life. On the other hand, its ideational phases are learned early and have persisted. The contradiction in the behavioral aspect may be given the same interpretation as that applied to twin births. We saw that the Niger Delta Pastorate repudiated both polygyny and twin infanticide, but was successful in gaining the cooperation of its members only as regards the latter. To the degree that infanticide is loosely integrated with other elements in Ijaw culture, polygyny is the reverse, being constantly supported by the values placed upon having children and an efficient household. We conclude, therefore, that polygyny, though practiced late in life, has remained stable because it is integrated with numerous other traits.

Everyone in Ebiama believes there has been an increase in sorcery (*diriguọ*). We find it difficult to estimate the intensity with which beliefs in *diriguọ* are held, even though Talbot in 1926 ascribed to the Ijaw "much" belief in "witchcraft" on a continuum between "excessive" and "slight" witchcraft that he found in other parts of Southern Nigeria (1926, II:20). The older men and women in the village reason that since the initiation of British administration there must be more sorcerers than formerly. As pointed out frequently in analyses of sorcery and witchcraft, the crucial issue is not whether magical practices are actually on the increase or even being practiced at all, but rather whether people believe they are. In pre-British times a person suspected of being a *diriguọkẹmẹ* could be subjected to an ordeal and, if proved guilty, would be killed or ostracized by his kinsmen. Under Nigerian law, ordeals are forbidden and a person can be fined for "defamation of character" for accusing someone of being a sorcerer. In consequence, the Ijaw maintain that more people have become *diriguoyou* because they have less fear of being exposed and punished.

Unlike the case of twin infanticide, polygyny, and the propitiation of *orumọ*, the church does not inveigh against the belief in sorcery. In Ebiama adults who have had the most years of schooling and are the sincerest Christians still maintain, without hesitation, the indigenous beliefs concerning the magical causes of seemingly accidental events. In school there are few attempts to teach an empirical method for approaching the natural world that would contradict the underlying premises of sorcery. If anything, the church and the school in this instance reinforce belief by identifying the villains of the Bible as *diriguọyou*. The belief in sorcery has thus remained an integral part of the Ijaw world view, satisfying the indigenous requirements for an explanation of unfortunate events while also becoming syncretized to the Christian concept of evil.

With traits held so tenaciously, the hypothesis of early learning would suggest that they are acquired very early in life. Yet, it has been noted that reference to *diriguọyou* are never used to frighten young children, and preadolescents between five and eight never consider their own illnesses to be the product of sorcery. Indeed, it is not until later that they explicitly fear sorcery, and refer knowingly to *diriguọyou* as evil characters in their stories. Sorcery, however, does not fall within our purview because the hypothesis of early learning applies only to situations in which there is a reason and an impetus for change. Early learning experiences of themselves cannot produce alternatives in culture. In this chapter we have examined the extent to which they help us understand the process whereby choices are made.

9/Conclusion

WE HAVE DESCRIBED EBIAMA as it was at the time of our study just prior to national independence. The isolation of the village allowed changes to filter in without sharp major disruptions to Ijaw culture or society. In these circumstances education was the adaptive mechanism for the community members to meet the future without being disabled by their past. This adaptation implies that the ideational traits of enculturation give meaning to and receive validation from the behavioral traits of socialization.

In the chart summarizing the data on the next page, the traits are numbered in the same order as first presented in Chapter 8. Support for the early learning hypothesis includes: (A) stable or persistent traits learned early in life—prior to the age of nine—and (B) traits acquired at a later age that are changing or have shown little resistance to change. The contradictory data are listed under: (C) labile traits acquired at an early age, and (D) stable traits learned late in life.

The distribution of traits in the Summary Chart helps us respond to the contradictory interpretations of the relationship between tenacity or instability and the type of trait. The Seminar on Acculturation assumes "concrete" (behavioral) traits tend to change more readily than "valuational" (ideational) ones during acculturation. The early learning hypothesis, however, posits those traits learned earliest, whether they be behavioral or not, will be most conservative. Since behavioral and ideational traits are fairly evenly divided in all columns of the chart, traits classified as part of enculturation do not appear to be any more or less stable than those attributed to socialization.

The early learning hypothesis purports to be only a partial explanation for differential rates of cultural and social change. Conversely, alternative explanations need not preclude references to the age of learning as a variable influencing the mutability of a trait. LeVine, for example, asserts that value orientations toward authority help explain why two structurally similar East African societies made dissimilar political adaptations to colonial administration. But he also finds the early learning hypothesis "lends plausibility" to the persistence and significance of political values for effecting different modes of political adjustment since they are learned early in childhood (LeVine 1960:57).

In a preliminary report on Ijaw enculturation (Leis 1964), the exceptions to the early learning hypothesis were related to the concept of overt culture or pattern. As defined by Kluckhohn, a pattern is "a structural regularity" for which there is "*articulate* awareness on the part of the culture carriers" (1941:112, 114). Unlike

SUMMARY CHART

	Learned Early	*Learned Late*

Stable Traits

A

1.a. Individualism and hard work are valued. (i)*

1.b. Girls practice women's tasks. (b)

4. Leadership is expressed informally with decisions based on group consensus. (b) (i)

5.a. Insults and assaults should be settled by force. (i)

9.a. Faith is expressed in power of *orumǫ.* (i)

12.a. Polygynous marriages are thought to be advantageous. (i)

D

8. Big-dowry wives are ritually punished for commiting adultery. (b) (i)

9.c. Taboos for *orumǫ* are practiced. (b)

12.b. Roles are acquired in polygynous marriages. (b)

Changing Traits

C

5.b. Feuds are redressed by force. (b)

10.a. Faith is held in ability of diviners. (i)

B

1.c. Youths practice men's tasks. (b)

2. Personal prestige is gained by acquiring certain kinds of possessions. (b) (i)

3. Matrilineal kinsmen acquire important legal status. (b) (i)

6. Definite amount of bridewealth must be paid. (b) (i)

7. Widows receive harsh treatment. (b) (i)

9.b. Propitiation of *orumǫ* includes personal participation. (b)

10.b. Diviners are sought at times of crisis. (b)

11. Twin births are destroyed. (b) (i)

---

* Type of trait:
  (b) behavioral
  (i) ideational

Malinowski's observation that "the natives obey the forces and commands of the tribal code, but they do not comprehend them . . .,"[1] our field research reveals that "the natives" are able to explain at least some of their acts and beliefs. We propose that it is of theoretical relevance whether people offer explanations merely in terms of custom, or whether they explicitly refer to the manifest functions of whatever it is they are trying to explain. Each of the traits learned late and remaining stable is interrelated by the Ijaw with a wide range of behavior and values, many of

---

[1] B. Malinowski, *Argonauts of the Western Pacific,* New York: E. P. Dutton & Company, 1961 (orig. pub. 1922), p. 11.

which are relatively untouched by acculturation. Traits, in other words, are integrated or non-integrated in patterns to the extent that they are consciously validated. The Ijaw have reasons for why a big-dowry wife must be punished for committing adultery, why taboos surrounding *orumǫ* should be respected, and why polygynous marriages should continue in the face of admonitions by church officials. These reasons constitute an intellectual network of self-support and provide stability for constituent traits. Change may still occur when traits of this sort are brought into direct conflict with a set of traits accepted during acculturation. Belief in the power of the local deities to cause unforeseen and calamitous events, for example, ties in with the act of propitiating carved figures, which creates a confrontation with the rationale of patterns involved in being a Christian. Here the age of learning may be seen to play a part in whether an Ijaw convert will begin to propitiate the *orumǫ* again once illness strikes his family and he must try to interpret and ameliorate its cause. Compared to a person with little schooling, an individual educated from an early age in the missionary school may be less likely to believe that the *orumǫ* require offerings before any other remedy will be effective.

The other negative cases, those traits in the category of learned early but lacking tenacity, either have little interrelationship with other traits—they are without intellectual reinforcement—or they may not have been actually abandoned. Government restrictions have apparently brought an end to armed conflicts as a means of settling disputes. The pattern of retaliation remains a part of Ijaw thought, however, and given the proper instigation it would not be surprising if feuding reappears in the future. A disregard of diviners by Christians is in keeping with the traditional view that most diviners are fakes to begin with, but more importantly, a visit to a diviner would inevitably result in a prophecy that an *oru* demands propitiation. Unless a convert wishes to compromise his new religion, therefore, he will avoid diviners and profess to disbelieve them.

Utilizing the concept of pattern *ex post facto* helps to explain the exceptions to the early learning hypothesis in the Ijaw case, but we acknowledge its inherent tautology: patterns can be interpreted as deriving from the integration of traits equally as much as the integration of a trait is related to a pattern. It is the combination of pattern with the age of learning that enables us to predict the degree of stability of a trait. Given the pervasive importance of the pattern of retaliation and its early learning, the possibility of a return to feuding seems likely. For the same reason, the emphases on individualism and being able to choose freely among alternatives suggest that more men and women will engage in trading because of the latitude open to individual achievement in this occupation should surpluses develop or traveling conditions improve. A final example of how the proposed interpretations offer predictable courses of change may be seen in the Ijaw belief in sorcery. On the basis of its conscious integration with other traits in Ijaw thought, its relevancy to the world view involving contrapuntal themes of individualism and fate, and its late learning, we can predict that should a stimulus for change arise in the future, the belief in sorcery will remain stable.

We have attempted to demonstrate the importance of childhood learning for cultural and social change in two ways. First, the age of learning Ijaw traits, in accordance with the early learning hypothesis, affects the tenacity or instability of a majority of traits during acculturation. Second, the content of education, including both enculturation and socialization, also affects differential rates of change to the extent of stabilizing traits perceived by the Ijaw as being integrated in patterns. The Ijaw emphasis on "free" choice and the equalitarian nature of social relationships typify the context by which education can offer both the alternatives and the limitations to action. These conclusions represent two forms of explanation: the first is analytical, based on our interpretation of factors that are extraneous to the Ijaws' perceptions but influence their selection of one alternative rather than another. The second acknowledges the importance of cognition and intention whereby individuals alter their social environment by conscious choices.

Glossary

IJAW WORDS

ama; *amananawei* or *amayanabo* (pl. *amananayou*): Village; village head.
ayoroba: Newlywed girl.
biyę krǫ: Powerful or resolute personality.
bonara; *bonawei*: Sister; brother.
bouyei; *bouyou*: Forest things; forest people.
burokęmę (pl. *buroyou*): Diviner.
dau; *dauwari*: Father or father's brother; father's agnates or father's residence.
dilę: Sorry.
dirigụǫ; diriguǫkęmę (pl. *diriguǫyou*): Sorcery, sorcerer.
dǫghǫ: Brother's wife or husband's siblings.
duwoiyou: Ancestors or ghosts.
egheriyo; *egherifa*: Story; end of story.
fę ęrę: "Big-dowry" (high bridewealth) wife.
foun (pl. *founyou*): Vampire.
ibe; *ibenanawei*: Clan, or nonunilineal descent group; clan chief.
iyei: "Something."
iyǫlǫli: Masseur or "presser."
kala amata: Married woman without children.
kala ikiya: "Small-dowry" (low bridewealth) wife.
kala tǫbou: Young child.
kęnę daubǫ; *kęnę nyinmǫ*: Half-siblings with same father; full or half-siblings with same mother.
kǫnu tǫbǫu: First-born child.
krǫ: Power.
ndo pęlę: Weaning.
noao: Thank you, or term of greeting.
nyinghi, nęnę; *nyinghi wari*: Mother or mother's sister; mother's uterine kinsmen or mother's (pre-marriage) residence.
obębę: Ladder, or divining instrument.
okoka pogholo: Ceremony for a delayed birth.
olotu: War leader or champion wrestler.
opudau; *opunyinghi*: Grandfather; grandmother.
opuduwoiyou: Ancestors who founded the village or who were great-grandparents.
oru (pl. *orumǫ*): Local deity, especially one residing in the forest.
owu (pl. *owumǫ*): Local deity residing in water, and/or masks for masquerade dance.
ozu ęnini: Shame.
ǫgǫ: Sister's husband or wife's siblings.
ǫvuǫ: Covenant.
sei diri: Poison.
su: Inadequate, inefficient, or lazy.

109

tẹmẹ: Soul.

tẹnẹbomo: Ceremony performed for boy cutting down his first bunch of palm fruits.

tọro krọ: Demonstrative personality.

wari: House, or nonunilineal descent group, or village section.

Wọnyinghi: Creator.

yabẹ: Mother's brother.

yei; yei nyinghi; yei dau: Husband; mother-in-law; father-in-law.

yeibinitẹiyara: Girl at age of agreeing to marry.

zifa: Barren woman.

zi pẹrẹ tọbọu: Uterine kinsman able to be sold to pay debts.

ziyara: Woman who has recently born a child.

zi ogbo: Age-group.

ANTHROPOLOGICAL TERMS

AFFINES: Kinsmen related by marriage.

AGNATIC KINSMEN: Persons related to each other through males.

BILATERAL KINSHIP: A form of kinship whereby individuals trace their relationship through males and females equally without emphasizing descent from a common ancestor. This form is typical of the United States.

BRIDEWEALTH: The wealth given by an Ijaw man to his bride's parents to obtain certain marital rights: domestic, economic, and sexual. With a large payment (a "big-dowry" marriage) an Ijaw also gains the right to make his wife's children members exclusively of his own kin groups.

CLAN: A group of persons who believe themselves linked through common descent. Under British rule clans were defined as territorial units and common residence became the basis for Ijaw clan membership.

CONSANGUINEALS: Kinsmen related by descent.

LEVIRATE: The practice of a woman marrying the brother of her deceased husband.

LINEAGE: A group of persons linked together through traceable descent to a common ancestor reckoned exclusively through only one sex. A patrilineage links individuals through males; a matrilineage through females.

NONUNILINEAL DESCENT GROUP: (Unrestricted:) All the descendants of a particular person, living or dead. (Restricted:) In the Ijaw case, choice of residence restricts membership to those descendants of a common ancestor living together.

PATRILOCAL: A type of residence rule whereby after marriage the couple reside near the husband's father.

SORCERER: A person who uses substances or acts in a supernatural way to cause harm to another person. Unlike a witch, the sorcerer's power is not innate but rather lies in the sorcerer's use of objects or of his performance itself.

SORORAL POLYGYNY: A type of marriage in which a man marries two or more women who are sisters.

SORORATE: The practice of a man marrying the sister of his deceased wife.

USUFRUCT: The right of an individual to use land belonging to his group.

UTERINE KINSMEN: Persons related to each other through females.

UXORILOCAL: A type of residence rule whereby after marriage the couple reside at the wife's residence.

VIRILOCAL: A type of residence rule whereby after marriage the couple reside at the husband's residence.

WITCH: A person with inherent supernatural power who uses it, not always consciously, to cause harm to another person.

Bibliography

ALAGOA, EBIEGBERI J., 1964, *The Small Brave City-State*. Madison: University of Wisconsin Press.

A history of Nembe Clan, one of the eastern Delta Ijaw city-states.

BRUNER, EDWARD W., 1956, "Cultural Transmission and Cultural Change." *Southwestern Journal of Anthropology* 12, 2:191–199.

A formulation and test of the early learning hypothesis using data from an American Indian group.

DIKE, K. ONWUKA, 1956, *Trade and Politics in the Niger Delta, 1830–1885*. Oxford: Clerendon Press.

The history of the rise and fall of Ijaw city-states during their last period of sovereignty.

FORTES, M., 1938, "Social and Psychological Aspects of Education in Taleland." Supplement to *Africa* 11, 4. London.

A study of the role of education and learning processes among the Tallensi of Ghana.

HENRY, JULES, 1960, "A Cross-Cultural Outline of Education." *Current Anthropology* 1, 4:267–305.

Proposal for standardizing cross-cultural comparisons of education.

HERSKOVITS, MELVILLE J., 1947, *Man and His Works*. New York: Alfred A. Knopf.

General anthropology text containing a discussion of why the concept of enculturation is important for understanding cultural stability and change.

HORTON, ROBIN, 1960, *The Gods as Guests*. Lagos: Nigeria Magazine.

A description, with photographs, of masquerade dancers in Kalabari Clan, one of the eastern Delta Ijaw city-states.

IKIME, OBARO, 1967, "The Western Ijǫ, 1900–1950: A Preliminary Study." *Journal of the Historical Society of Nigeria* 4, 1:65–87.

An account of the adaptation to colonial control by the western Delta clans.

JONES, G. I., 1963, *The Trading States of the Oil Rivers*. London: Oxford University Press.

A political and economic history of the eastern Delta Ijaw city-states.

KLUCKHOHN, CLYDE, 1941, "Patterning as Exemplified in Navaho Culture." In L. Spier, A. I. Hallowell, and S. S. Newman (eds.), *Language, Culture, and Personality*, pp. 109–130. Menasha, Wisc.: Sapir Memorial Publication Fund.

Definitions of pattern and other related concepts.

LEIS, PHILIP E., 1964, "Ijaw Enculturation: A Reexamination of the Early Learning Hypothesis." *Southwestern Journal of Anthropology* 20, 1:32–42.

A summary statement interpreting differential cultural change in the Ijaw village that is described here.

————, 1965, "The Nonfunctional Attributes of Twin Infanticide in the Niger Delta." *Anthropological Quarterly* 38:97–111.

The consequences of nonfunctional customs for interpreting culture change are discussed in relation to Ijaw twin infanticide.

LEONARD, ARTHUR G., 1906, *The Lower Niger and Its Tribes.* London: Macmillan & Co.

An early description of the Ijaw with emphasis on their religious beliefs.

LEVINE, ROBERT A., 1960, "The Internalization of Political Values in Stateless Societies." *Human Organization* 19:51–58.

A comparative approach to explaining the different adaptations made by two structurally similar East African societies to colonial rule.

LEWIS, L. J., 1965, *Society, Schools and Progress in Nigeria.* London: Pergamon Press.

An analysis of the roles of formal education and schools in pre- and post-independent Nigeria and their possible functions in the future.

MEAD, MARGARET, 1963, "Socialization and Enculturation." *Current Anthropology* 4, 2:184–188.

A brief statement defining the two terms.

OWONARO, S. K., 1949, *The History of Ijo (Ijaw).* Lagos.

An accumulation of local clan histories combined with speculation on the origin of the Ijaw as a whole.

RAUM, OTTO, 1940, *Chaga Childhood.* London: Oxford University Press.

A detailed account of educational practices in an East African society.

READ, MARGARET, 1959, *Children of Their Fathers.* London: Methuen and Company.

Description of childhood in a Central African society.

SHIMAHARA, NOBUO, 1970, "Enculturation—A Reconsideration." *Current Anthropology* 11, 2:143–154.

This theoretical statement argues that enculturation should be defined as a dynamic life-long transaction between an individual and his culture.

SPIRO, MELFORD E., 1955, "The Acculturation of American Ethnic Groups." *American Anthropologist* 57, 6:1240–1252.

A discussion of the early learning hypothesis along with other explanations for interpreting acculturation in the United States.

TALBOT, P. AMAURY, 1926, *The Peoples of Southern Nigeria.* London: Oxford University Press. 4 vols.

———, 1932, *Tribes of the Niger Delta.* London: Sheldon Press.

Summary of most of what was known about the Ijaw by the time of the publication of these works.

WELCH, J. W., 1937, *The Isoko Clans of the Niger Delta.* Ph.D. Dissertation. Cambridge University.

Description and history of an ethnic group neighboring the western Delta Ijaw.

WOLFE, ALVIN W., 1961, *In the Ngombe Tradition.* Evanston, Ill.: Northwestern University Press.

Ethnography of a Congo ethnic group provides a resumé of several interpretations of social and cultural change.